SUCCESS
secrets to maximize
BUSINESS
in
CANADA

Ken Coates

TIMES BOOKS INTERNATIONAL
Singapore • Kuala Lumpur

National Library Board (Singapore) Cataloguing in Publication Data

Coates, Ken.
    Success secrets to maximise business in Canada/Ken Coates.--
Times Books International, 2001.
        p. cm. -- (Culture shock!)
        Includes bibliography and index
        ISBN: 981-232-161-6

1. Business etiquette--Canada 2. Corporate culture--Canada 3. Success in
business--Canada I. Title II. Series: Culture Shock!

HF5389
395.5209710648--dc21

                                                    SLS2001005078

Photographs are by Les Holroyd, Vancouver, British Columbia

© 2001 Times Media Private Limited
Published by Times Books International
An imprint of Times Media Private Limited
A member of the Times Publishing Group
Times Centre, 1 New Industrial Road, Singapore 536196
Fax: (65)285 4871 Tel: (65)284 8844
e-mail:te@tpl.com.sg

Online Bookstore:
http://www.timesone.com.sg/te

Times Subang
Lot 46, Subang Hi-Tech Industrial Park
Batu Tiga
40000 Shah Alam
Selangor Darul Ehsan
Malaysia
Fax & Tel: (603)736 3517
e-mail:cchong@tpl.com.my

Printed in Singapore

ISBN 981 232 161 6

Contents

Introduction

Hewers of Wood and Drawers of Water: Myths and Images of Canadian Business

Canada has an identity crisis. Alongside an intense, never-ending internal struggle to define the national character, the country battles with a contradictory international image. On one hand, there is the annual commentary on the United Nations Human Development Index, a well-publicized report which has, for eight straight years, ranked Canada as the best country in the world in which to live. Offsetting this, however, is the reality of living cheek by jowl with the world's last remaining superpower, a situation guaranteed to produce a problem with national self-confidence. Is Canada the world's best nation, or a poor imitation of the United States? Moreover, is it a promising, high-tech economy, poised to lead the world in the implementation of the Internet, or is it a declining resource-based nation, as yet unable to cope with the competitive realities of the age of globalization?

Historically, the country is well-known for its staggering resource potential. Canada has produced boatloads of furs and fish, countless stands of commercial timber, vast mineral wealth, and the bounty from thousands of small farms. It is a nation defined, at least in the public's eye, by its mines, logging camps and fishing villages. Canada's rural and resource past lingers as an indelible part of its contemporary image, aided by an international tourism campaign which promotes the country's vast open spaces, wildlife, and rustic, pioneering spirit. Canada is a land of mountains, Mounties (Royal Canadian Mounted Police) and moose—an endearing image which plays well in the travel brochures but which contradicts the country's claims to be an aggressive, technologically proficient competitor in the global economy.

The Canadian reality is a bit of everything. The mines still operate—and occasionally touch off enormous international interest, as did the recent discovery of diamonds in the North. Logging camps are more high-tech than in the past, feeding the voracious appetites of some of the world's most modern pulp and paper mills and hundreds of sawmills producing for the US, Asian and European markets. The fishing villages have been in decline for decades, their vitality sapped by years of over-fishing and questionable resource management practices. But still, along the Atlantic and Pacific coasts, the boats and ships continue to head out to sea, returning with their catch to keep the fish plants and processors in business for yet another year. Prairie farming may have lost the romance of oxen-pulled plows, and air-conditioned harvesters may lack the appeal of the sickle, but Canada's wheat belt continues to produce vast quantities of high quality grain for the world market.

But Canada is also extremely modern. Its major urban economies—Vancouver, Calgary, Edmonton, Toronto, Ottawa and Montreal—are tied into the high technology world of the global economy. These centers harbor rich multi-cultural communities, with the entrepreneurial spirit sustained by regular infusions of immigrants from Asia, Africa, the Caribbean, South America and Europe. These dynamic and fast-growing centers dominate the nation's economy and, increasingly, political life. Often criticized by the rural areas, which face continued decline and economic hardships, Canada's major cities are internationally competitive and, in select sectors, world leaders. Images of Toronto's Harbourside, Montreal's Old Town, Calgary's Olympic facilities, Edmonton's famous shopping center or Vancouver's rich Asian character occasionally make their way into the tourism brochures, but this is not the Canada that most travelers anticipate.

This is a country, too, with strong international connections. This can be seen at the airports, where thousands of travelers a day arrive from around the world to visit the country's major tourist attractions—the world's best skiing in Whistler, B.C., the famous Banff-Jasper Rocky Mountain corridor, or Niagra Falls — to connect up to one of the country's many international companies, or to visit relatives. Global influences are readily apparent in the restaurant and cultural scenes in the major cities, on-going proof of the unique and peaceful vitality of Canadian multiculturalism. More careful observers will find evidence in the business pages, where foreign companies demonstrate their continuing interest and confidence in the Canadian economy through their investments in major national firms or through sizable contracts with Canadian companies. Canada is a country with strong financial ties around the world, most notably with the United States, Britain, Japan, Hong Kong, China and Germany.

Foreign interest is not an unvarnished blessing, however, and observers will find that it takes little to scratch Canadian sensitivities on this score. Over the past decade, international firms have found Canadian companies very attractive and the shifting locus of economic control—from Canadian to foreign hands—has some people quite nervous. In Vancouver and Toronto, where vast amounts of Hong Kong money came during the years leading up to the transfer of the crown colony to China, there is abundant evidence of overseas capital. So, too, can it be seen in Alberta's oil patch, in Ontario's bustling and critical automobile sector, and in many other parts of the country. Even Quebec, home to a large majority of the country's French Canadian population and long a bastion of economic nationalism (in this case, provincialism), there are increasing signs that foreign investors find the region's businesses attractive.

Canada's uncertainty about the future is deeply embedded in its past. It has, since its establishment as an almost-independent nation in 1867, lived in the shadows of the empire. In the mid-19th century, Canada was a colonial dependency of Great Britain. Unlike the United States, the colonies rested quite easily under the mantle of Queen Victoria and there was no grand public agitation for independence or separation from the empire. Confederation left Canada with strong ties to Britain, ones that survived the sacrifices of World War I and World War II. The veritable destruction of Britain during World War II left the mother country with significantly reduced international authority. Canada had, it seemed, a perfect opportunity to step out from the Imperial umbrella and establish true international independence.

The country tried, but the security of British protection was traded, in the early days of the Cold War, for the certainty of US military coverage. Canada strove to establish a separate international presence—its superb diplomatic corps attempted in the 1950s to give meaning to the concept of "Middle Power" diplomacy—but the presence of the US colossus gave quick lie to Canadian aspirations for meaningful separation. The country benefited from closer economic ties with the United States, particularly during the great industrial boom of the 1950s and 1960s, but many Canadians found the reliance on US military protection to be only a sad substitute for colonial subservience to Great Britain.

Over time, however, the connections between Canada and the United States became stronger and more complex. Over 90% of all Canadians live within 250 kilometers of the Canada–US boundary—and most of Canada's population live below the 49th parallel—the symbolic border line between the country (but only the actual boundary in the western half of the nation). Brief flirtations with economic nationalism in the 1960s through the 1980s demonstrated the impracticality of Canadian economic distinctiveness, and resulted in the country's surprisingly quiet acceptance of the Canada–US Free Trade Agreement in 1988 (later the North America Free Trade Agreement, when Mexico joined in 1994). Canada shared, a tad belatedly and less dramatically, in the technology-inspired US boom of the 1990s, and endured the sorry sight of seeing many of its leading entrepreneurs and skilled personnel moving south for the higher wages, lower taxes, and greater opportunities to be found in the United States. Not surprisingly, therefore, many people around the world see Canada as little more than a cold, northward extension of the United States, rich in resources, but saddled with a more interventionist government and a less dynamic business environment. While there is some truth to these assumptions—just as there is substance underlying the global stereotype of Canada as a land of snow, polar bears and hockey players—there is far more to this complex and dynamic country than these images suggest. The specifics of the Canadian business environment will be described in the following chapters, but rest assured that the full story is well-worth reading.

Canada is well-placed to capitalize on the opportunities and challenges of the global economy. This, of course, is no assurance that the country will respond well and creatively to the issues before it. But consider, first, the positive side of the ledger. The country is home to recent immigrants from around the world. Some, particularly from Asia, came with money and commercial contacts. Most brought intense entrepreneurial energy and determination. They offer connections to the developed and emerging economies of the world, and present a unique opportunity to transform a parochial, US-centered business community into a global force. The country has, as well, a highly-trained, reliable and hard-working work force, a bit low on technical expertise but generally adaptable and determined. Canada brings to the table enormous quantities of raw materials and energy resources: wheat and other grains, timber, minerals, hydro-electric power, oil and natural gas. It can claim, with justification, to having incubated some technologically world class companies, ranging from Bombardier to JDS Uniphase and Nortel, and to being a world-leader in telecommunications. It has a stable political system (check out how Canada handles its major separatist movement) and a strong banking and financial system (although, oddly, the technical difficulties of the computer system underpinning the Toronto Stock Exchange has been a source of considerable embarrassment). Add to this a strategic position next to the United States of America and beautifully placed between Europe and Asia and one sees all of the preconditions for economic prosperity and, indeed, leadership in international trade.

There is, of course, another side. Canada's once vaunted social welfare system has been cut back dramatically, particularly in health care, leaving the country saddled with a worrisome debt burden. While some areas of the nation prosper from the new economy and access to the US market, others falter and languish far behind, propped up by federal transfer payments. Canada has a persistently high unemployment rate, serious difficulties with the First Nations (aboriginal) population, continued tension over Quebec separation (and growing unease in western Canada that merits close attention), and some major environmental difficulties, not the least of which is the collapse of the east coast cod fishery. The country's rich resources—long the foundation for a strong, working and middle class economy—have been rendered less attractive by the forces of global competition. The high wages in the resource and industrial sector, similarly, have made some sectors less competitive internationally.

Canada was almost a great nation, agonizingly close to becoming a permanent fixture at the top of the world's financial tables. But while it has held its own with regard to the social indicators, the country's financial fortunes have faltered. The Canadian dollar has plummeted relative to the US dollar, raising the cost of living (while keeping many companies and sectors alive) and adding to the income and standard of living gap between Canada and the United States. Canadian stocks, save for a few high-flyers (that lost a lot of ground late in 2000), languished relative to the vibrant US market. Canadian taxes remain considerably higher than in the United States, although the size of the gap is often exaggerated by critics of government policy. The country has suffered, too, from uneven political leadership.

Brokerage politics work in Canada—Canadians loved to be bribed by their tax dollars—and the country has routinely shied away from major initiatives designed to address deeply entrenched economic, administrative or social issues. Even the country's now-celebrated budgetary surplus owes far more to the strength of the US economy—and therefore unexpected government revenues—than to any dramatic or creative leadership on the part of federal or provincial politicians. Add to this the social tensions, political difficulties, regional economic inequalities, and other challenges and you find a country that is, at once, optimistic and pessimistic. And that, perhaps, is the best way to understand Canada—a nation with enormous potential, some truly world class companies, serious structural problems, vast resource potential (look at the country's fresh water supply), and poor political leadership.

The chapters that follow will explore the general character of Canada and the Canadian economy—for it is little known, even to international business people who do a lot of work in this country—and to the specifics of the Canadian business environment. The goal herein is to provide an overview of a potentially exciting and dynamic nation, one with a well-deserved reputation for civility and decency, and which possesses an unusually strong social conscience. Canada is a welcoming nation—open to immigrants, foreign investment, and travelers—and is far less demanding of newcomers than many other countries in the world. That it rests in the shadow of the United States, and that the United States is such a dominant economic force in the post-Cold War era, has stripped some of the lustre off the "true north, strong and free." But as you will see, the country is deserving of a careful and considered look. What you see might well surprise you; what you learn might well prepare you to capitalize on the exciting commercial opportunities to be found in one of the world's largest, most peaceful, safest, most decent, and richest nations.

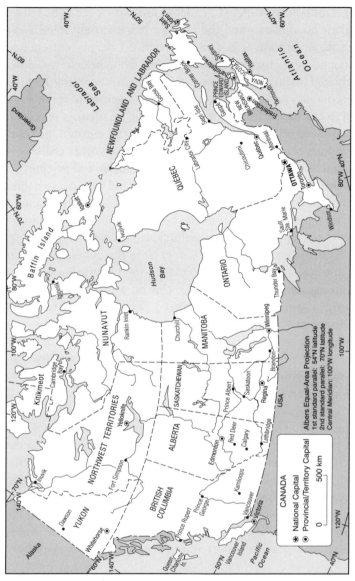

Map of Canada

CHAPTER 1

The Best Country in the World: Canada Described

For seven consecutive years, the United Nations Human Development Index has listed Canada as the best country in the world in which to live. Like any ranking system, this one is open to criticism—and, goodness knows, Canadians are good at self-criticism. But the HDI provides an unusually comprehensive measure of how a country is doing. GDP and per capita income statistics offer a gross and incomplete portrait of financial and economic health; the HDI looks at such factors as income, life expectancy, environmental protection, social services, housing, opportunities for women, respect for cultural diversity, and the like. For one country—any country—to consistently appear at the top of the tables is no small feat. It is hardly surprising, therefore, that Prime Minister Jean Chrétien routinely pulls out the HDI ranking when faced with criticism of Canada's economic or political performance. To be No. 1, year after year, suggests that the country is doing something right.

It is indicative of Canada, however, that the No. 1 rating does not mean that Canada is first in any particular category. Canada's skill lies in being mid to high range on all of the factors, thus winning on the averages. In some ways, this is a lovely metaphor for the country as a whole: a great place to live and work, not a bad economic and social environment, a middle power in virtually everything that it does. Canada, it seems, does well but not superbly, rarely a beacon of world leadership, but an impressive nation for its ability to find a balance in so many aspects of national life.

Canada: A Brief History

Critics of Canada—and they are almost all internal, as the rest of the world pays preciously little attention to a country that deserves far more recognition—worry that the country is due for a major economic and social shakedown. The concerns rest, in the main, on nervousness about the future of Canada's resource sectors. Since the first Europeans arrived in the area in the sixteenth century, the pursuit of natural resources has been the top economic priority. First Nations (indigenous people) have inhabited the land known as Canada for many centuries, tracing their ancestry back over 15,000 years. Vibrant and diverse societies emerged, each demonstrating a remarkable adaptation to their specific ecological zone. Subsistence was drawn from the land, providing for a lifestyle that was comfortable, sustainable and culturally rich.

The arrival of Europeans, each searching for the kind of wealth discovered by the Spanish and Portuguese in central and south America and each bringing missionaries determined to convert the "heathens" to Christianity, altered First Nations lives quite dramatically. The French and British did not find the great deposits of minerals and gems that they anticipated, but they did find ocean waters teeming with cod fish and forests filled with fur-bearing animals that produced pelts in abundance for an eager market in Europe. Early commerce and industry was generally limited and was controlled by a handful of large companies. Importantly, perhaps, the new territories figured prominently in British and French rivalries and a bitter contest over European control of eastern North America ensued. Only with the British conquest of New France (Quebec) in 1759–1760 was this contest finally settled, only to have the British see many of their remaining colonies rise up in a bloody revolt only a few years later.

The American revolution resulted, ultimately, in the creation of two nations. The United States emerged quickly after the fighting ended, a new union of former British colonies determined to bring republican principles to bear on life in the "New World."

Other colonies resisted what some viewed as the rise of "mobocracy" and opted for the security of the British Empire over the uncertainty of the experiment in radical democracy. These colonies include the former French stronghold of Quebec (along the Saint Lawrence River), Nova Scotia and Newfoundland on the Atlantic coast. None of the three colonies sided with the revolutionaries—although a few people in Nova Scotia and Quebec considered joining. At war's end, thousands of North American "Loyalists," unwilling or unable to rest their lot with the new American state, abandoned the south for the remaining British colonies. They arrived in droves, first to Nova Scotia and Quebec and, in later years, to the new colony of Upper Canada, north of the Great Lakes.

The combination of the existing population and the new migrants created a strongly British society—with even the French Canadians in Quebec throwing their lot in with the British—with strongly anti-American overtones. (Politics was, of course, not an accurate reflection of reality. Many of the Loyalists and so-called Late Loyalists came for reasons of convenience or personal opportunity, the latter stimulated by government land grants and offers of assistance to new settlers.) North America, therefore, now had two major population blocks: the United States (initially a group of 13 colonies along the Atlantic coast) and the area that was not the United States. British North America, to put it more positively, was united by a belief in British parliamentary democracy, affection for the monarchy and what scholars later called "the Tory touch," a small-"c" conservative orientation that favored social hierarchy (the "superiors" should rule) and placed the development of the collective over the celebration of individual rights. The British-French relationship was strained at times, with the French Canadians sitting uneasily within the British Empire and resisting assimilation into the new linguistic and social order. But British North America proved quite resilient, resisting American attacks during the War of 1812 (when British soldiers burned down the White House) and establishing a different political and social system than in the ever-expanding United States.

The northern colonies inched cautiously toward independence. Political and linguistic tensions in the 1830s resulted in small uprisings which threatened the stability of the colonies. Britain, by now less than enamoured with the cost and difficulty of managing the North American dependencies, merged Upper Canada (Ontario) and Lower Canada (Quebec) into the United Province of the Canadas. The Maritime region, which had been divided into three colonies (Prince Edward Island, Nova Scotia and New Brunswick), actually performed better than the Canadas, both economically and politically, and were Britain's prized possessions on the continent. Nova Scotian sailing ships were known the world over, and regional entrepreneurs and bankers were among the wealthiest in British North America. The Canadas, in contrast, wallowed in the mire of class and ethnic politics and faced growing economic difficulties, exacerbated by a runaway public debt.

The solution favored by a small cadre of politicians in the Canadas and by the British Colonial Office, was the union of the British North American colonies. The Canadas agreed, hoping that expansion would provide a larger tableau upon which they could address their internal difficulties. The Atlantic colonies, specially Newfoundland, were aloof, although pressure from political leaders and British appointees brought Nova Scotia and New Brunswick to the table, reluctant participants in the birth of a new nation. In 1867, the Dominion of Canada was formed, consisting of Nova Scotia, New Brunswick, Quebec and Ontario. As a sign of what lay ahead for the fledgling country, Prince Edward Island and Newfoundland rejected the appeal to join, and numerous separatist candidates from Nova Scotia and New Brunswick were elected to federal and provincial office at the earliest opportunity. This was, after, all a marriage of central Canadian convenience more than an act of affection and true loyalty.

Separatist impulses withered in due course (although some French Canadians remained uncertain about the new political entity), and the Dominion turned its attentions to the task of nation-building. The United States provided a useful role model, for by the 1860s, the large and prosperous country stretched from British North America to Mexico, from the Atlantic to the Pacific, and (following the purchase of Alaska from the Russians in 1867) from the Gulf of Mexico to the Arctic Ocean. US jingoism, encapsulated in the concept of "manifest destiny" (the belief that God had ordained the US to rule the continent), reached a fever pitch at the end of the American civil war and helped convince Canadians to accept Confederation. Now, the Canadian desire was to replicate the US expansionist accomplishment, to build a nation from coast to coast and to use western development to fuel economic growth.

The British government, still in control of the vast area known as Rupert's Land and the gold mining colonies of British Columbia and Vancouver Island on the west coast, encouraged the expansion of the Dominion of Canada to the west coast. They facilitated the purchase of Rupert's Land from the chartered Hudson's Bay Company, and supported efforts to convince the newly created colony of British Columbia (which now included Vancouver Island) to join. West coasters were reluctant. They had few ties with Canada, and their commerce ran North to South, not East to West. Moreover, the gold rush had brought thousands of Americans into the region, fueling local fears of US annexation. But the colony was open to bribes, and it came in the form of a promise to build a transcontinental railway and to carry out some major public works in the region. (Prince Edward Island was, likewise, bought into Confederation in 1873; the independent-minded folks of Newfoundland continued to resist British and Canadian entreaties and remained a separate Dominion until 1949.)

By 1873, the major contours of Canada had been set, but political compromises did not a nation make. Federal politicians

From Trading Posts to Department Stores

The Hudson's Bay Company is one of the world's oldest, continuously operating companies. It was founded under Royal Charter in 1670, and is still a major feature in the Canadian retail scene. The company carried British hopes in the competitive North American fur trade and operated initially out of a series of small posts on the forbidding shores of Hudson Bay. Inland expansion touched off competition with Montreal-based traders and resulted, in the early nineteenth century, in the merger of the HBC and its main rival, the North West Company. The Hudson's Bay Company changed with the times, becoming a major land holder and retailer during the settlement boom on the prairies. The firm maintained its northern fur trading operations well into the twentieth century, only divesting itself of its fur division and Northern Stores operations in the past two decades. Early in the twentieth century, the HBC (The Bay in English Canada and le Baie in Quebec) expanded its retail operations. Large, flagship department stores were opened in each of the country's major cities. The company's fortunes took a turn for the worse in the 1980s, a period of intense difficulty in the Canadian retail sector, forcing a consolidation and streamlining of its operations. The company's retail operations survived and, indeed, expanded through the purchase of lower end rivals.

had to keep their promise and build a railway, no small feat for a small and poor country, and they had to attract settlers onto the vast western plains in order to fulfil their dream of a prosperous, growing nation. A Metis (people of mixed aboriginal and French ancestry) uprising in the west in 1869-1870 spoiled the initial celebration, and the railway project foundered in the face of massive construction problems and mounting debt. The railway had, after all, to cross thousands of miles of sparsely settled wilderness, much of it across the vaunted and forbidding Canadian shield north of the Great Lakes. Equally, the Canadian Pacific Railway, as the private firm charged with building the railway was called, had to build through the impressive Rocky and Coastal mountain ranges. The railway came close to bankruptcy on more than one occasion, only to be bailed out by a Canadian government which believed that its political fortunes and the future of the country rested on the completion of the project. Even a second Metis uprising in 1885 could not stop the project, which was finally completed that same year.

Prosperity did not immediately follow the completion of the railway. In fact, the United States continued to attract most of the potential settlers, including goodly numbers of migrants out of Ontario and Quebec (who headed primarily for the industrial towns in the northeastern US). Only in the late 1890s, when the American west began to run out of free land and when European countries opened the floodgates to permit more emigration, did the promise of Canada begin to come to fruition. Hundreds of thousands of farmers flowed out of Europe, including many released from Russia and the Ukraine, and onto the western plains. Towns and cities sprang up and dueled for urban supremacy, new railways were built, and agricultural production skyrocketed (aided by major improvements in agricultural science and dry-land farming equipment). Prairie settlement, in turn, fueled an industrial boom in central Canada. Factories in Ontario and Quebec, protected by sizable tariffs barriers designed to keep out cheaper US products, dispatched trainloads of supplies to the western farmers. Those same trains returned to the east loaded with the products from the rich farmlands of the western plains.

Canada in the Twentieth Century

Canada changed profoundly in the years between 1896 and 1914. The country's ethnic composition shifted as Eastern Europeans were added to the English and French populations. Asians and southern Europeans (particularly Italians) were recruited to work as cheap labor on railway projects and many chose to stay in the country when the projects wound down. Divisions emerged between a growing and ill-paid industrial working class, a smaller group of skilled workers and the country's still tiny entrepreneurial and political elite. Westerners discovered that the rich soils of the prairie did not fully compensate for the political injustices (central Canadian control and the manipulation of government policy in favor of the east) embedded in Confederation and lobbied for the creation of new provinces. Three were created: Manitoba in 1871, and Saskatchewan and Alberta in 1905. Western agitation continued, however, as easterners dominated the political system and used their clout to ensure the passage of legislation favorable to the protected industries of central Canada. The Maritime colonies suffered as well. The post-Confederation years saw a quick bleeding away of the region's entrepreneurial spirit and capital, and the loss of major industries to technological change (metal ships replaced wooden vessels) and government policies which favored central Canada. Canada did not match the United States in wealth or accomplishment—and continued to see itself as but a pale imitation of its more famous neighbor. But compared to other nations at a similar stage of development—New Zealand, Australia, Argentina, Brazil or South Africa—the country had made major strides and seemed destined to take a significant role in economic and political affairs.

Canada's coming of age occurred during World War I. As an integral part of the British Empire, Canada was automatically at war with Germany and its allies the moment that Great Britain declared war in 1914. The country responded with unparalleled enthusiasm. Tens of thousands of young men, many of them recent immigrants from Britain, rushed to arms and filled the ranks of the Canadian Expeditionary Force. The nation's industries mobilized for an all-out war effort, with Canada emerging as a key British ally in the years leading up to the United States entry into the war in 1917. The horrors of the conflict exacted a heavy toll from Canada, however, as Allied officers sent wave upon wave of young men into the blistering gunfire from the German trenches. Commentators came to believe that Canadian nationalism was forged on the battlefields of the western front during World War I. For sure, the conflict built Canadian confidence and assertiveness. In the postwar years, the country assumed an independent stance in world diplomacy and slowly weaned itself from its British parent.

By war's end, Canada had earned itself a promising international reputation. Three transcontinental trains crossed the nation, several million farmers toiled on the soil of the western plains, Ontario and Quebec boasted a growing industrial base, sheltered from global and US competition by high tariff walls. The country's bountiful resource wealth—east coast and west fisheries, countless acres of harvestable timber, dozens of rich mineral deposits—joined with a determined working class to give Canada entry into world markets. Manufacturing served only national consumers, with a small export trade to the US and Great Britain, but continued prosperity offered the promise that industrial production would, in time, be internationally competitive. Although the country still struggled in the shadow of Britain and was not accorded full recognition as a major world player, Canada's progress toward full national status seemed assured.

The promise of the immediate post-World War I period was not realized for a very long time. The boom of the 1920s proved as illusory in Canada as in the US. The US stock market crash and the resulting Great Depression sapped the vitality out of the Canadian economy. Tens of thousands of workers were thrown out of their jobs; many took to the rails, jumping freight trains to crisscross the country in pursuit of work. An ecological crisis on the great plains reached north into Canada, creating an enormous dust bowl on the formerly fertile plains and wreaking havoc with prairie agriculture. Farmers struggled to hold on to their farms; many thousands gave up in despair and joined the growing food lines in the major cities. Canada's fragile confidence took a beating, for the country was still uncertain about its short and long-term prospects. Political unrest spread across the land, producing all manner of left and right wing protest parties, each promising to end the depression and return hope to the country.

The economic crisis ended only when another began. The onset of World War II pulled thousands out of the ranks of the unemployed and into military uniform. Canada found itself, once again, as Britain's principal ally. Remembering the carnage of World War I, the Canadian government did not press its troops into action right away, but it did devote the country's industrial plant to the Allied war effort. The unemployed who were not yet in the armed forces found work in the hundreds of reopened and expanded factories. All manner of military equipment came off Canadian assembly lines, and sustained the British war effort during that nation's darkest hour. The intensity and importance of the Canadian contribution was soon obscured by the US entry into the war in December 1941—once again, Canada found itself taking a back seat to its more powerful and globally influential southern neighbor.

The Emergence of Modern Canada

In the years following World War II, Canada took a more prominent place in world affairs. It suffered, still, from comparisons to the United States—more dynamic, wealthier, and with a much larger population—but the country began to make more of a name for itself. Canadians played critical roles in the establishment of the United Nations and the country presented itself to the world as a Middle Power, betwixt Great Britain and the United States, the United States and Russia, and the industrialized rich nations and the poorer, underdeveloped countries of the world. Canadian diplomats pioneered the concept of international peacekeeping (Lester Pearson, later Canada's Prime Minister, received the Nobel Peace Prize for his work during the Suez crisis in the 1950s) and established an enviable reputation for decency and reliability in world affairs. Some, including many Canadians, worried that the nation slept too comfortably under the US military umbrella—an increasingly important issue as the Cold War unfolded—but the concept of Canada began to mean more and more on the international stage.

Nation-building continued as well. Newfoundland was brought into Confederation, reluctantly and only after two referendums, in 1949. The vast northern districts—the Yukon and Northwest Territories evolved more slowly, in part because of their small population and because the federal government wished to control regional resources. Protests resulted in the gradual extension of local administration, and the territories became self-governing in the late 1970s. One of the most high profile initiatives came in 1999, when Canada celebrated the establishment of Nunavut, created by dividing the Northwest Territories in two. Nunavut is unique both for its Arctic location and the fact that over 90% of its population is indigenous. The Inuit (formerly known as Eskimo) people of the region will, through Nunavut, exercise considerable authority over their economic and social development, representing one of the world's most important efforts at indigenous self-government. (The remaining part of the Northwest Territories has engaged in a lengthy debate about the name for the other half of the old jurisdiction. When a local media outlet asked the public to vote for their favorite, the winning name was "Bob." Surprisingly, this name has not yet been formally adopted—but who says Canadians don't have a sense of humor.)

Canadian confidence grew dramatically during the 1960s, in part because of unprecedented economic expansion and increased personal wealth and in part due to the social conflicts that engulfed the United States in this decade. Canada stood aloof from US involvement in Vietnam (save for sharing in sizable economic benefits from military procurement) and was sharply critical of the US war effort. The country opened its doors to US draft dodgers, and recoiled in horror at the race riots that accompanied the effort to expand civil rights in the US (even though its own record was far from pristine). This period saw, as well, the expansion of the Canadian welfare state, including the introduction of a much-vaunted national health care scheme and extensive regional economic development initiatives. In the year of Canada's centennial, 1967, the country engaged in an uncharacteristic celebration of national accomplishments and reveled in its emergence as a significant economic and political power. The following year, the charismatic Pierre Eliot Trudeau swept into the Prime Minister's office on the back of an outpouring of enthusiasm and confidence in the country's future.

The joy proved to be short-lived. The 1970s saw a soaring national debt, unrestrained government spending, and runaway inflation. Whatever solace Canadians found in the United State's continued difficulties—the loss of the Vietnam war, the forced resignation of the disgraced President Richard Nixon, and continued racial tensions south of the border—was eroded by the reality of high unemployment, profound economic difficulties, and growing political unrest. The capstone of the country's trials came in 1976 with the election of the separatist Parti Quebecois in the Province of Quebec. This represented the greatest threat to date to the once-more fragile Confederation. Indigenous groups, likewise, demanded more attention to their social and economic ills and insisted on recognition of their legal rights. Canadian multiculturalism, established as a national political priority, generated growing frustration among some sections of the population. Most significantly, the social compact embedded in the Canadian welfare state seemed threatened by the failure of federal and provincial programs to arrest the country's continued slide.

Over the past twenty years, the federal government slowly got its fiscal house in order. It did so by shifting programs to the provincial level, by cutting the size of government, and by increasing taxes. In a hotly debated move which dominated the 1988 federal election campaign (but which attracted scarcely a ripple of interest south of the border), the government of Prime Minister Brian Mulroney negotiated a Canada-US Free Trade

Agreement, designed to lower trade barriers between the two countries. The United State's remarkable economic performance, particularly through the 1990s, and the arrival of the information technology boom filtered across the Canada-US border and brought something of a return to prosperity in Canada. The economic recovery was uneven, far stronger in Ontario and Alberta than the Maritimes, for example, but the country's high unemployment rate dropped, by century's end, to a manageable seven per cent.

Canada is a peaceful, gentle nation, which continues to welcome hundreds of thousands of immigrants each year. It is a truly multicultural country; the major cities of Vancouver, Toronto and Montreal, in particular, are international models of cultural accommodation and cooperation. The economy, while not even across the land, is strong and relatively innovative. Canada enjoys a significant role on the world stage. It remains active in peacekeeping activities, is known for its social conscience, and continues to offer itself as a broker between rich and poor countries. While the country has issues to address (to be discussed below), it is a formidable, decent, comfortable place, blessed with enormous physical beauty, bountiful resources, and a diverse and talented population. Clearly, the United Nations Human Development Index is onto something when, year after year, it ranks Canada as the world's best nation.

Conditions and Challenges

Canada is the world's second largest nation, behind only Russia. (The country is guilty of the minor offense of "mapism." It has long loved the fact—much as Britain, in its heyday, loved the maps of the Empire—that Canada sits so prominently on the globe.) The country covers five time zones (Newfoundland, the brunt of endless jokes in Canada, has a time zone that is half an hour ahead of Atlantic Canada) and stretches from the Atlantic to the Pacific and from the southern tip of Ontario to the high Arctic. The

Canada is noted for its ethnic diversity. As this advertisement for an East Indian performance

country's geography is incredibly varied, incorporating the ancient and eroded hills of the east, the dominating solidity of the vast Canadian Shield, hundreds of miles of open prairie, vast tundra lands in the Arctic, the majestic mountain ranges of Alberta and British Columbia, and the prominent river valleys of the far north, including the Yukon and the Mackenzie.

Arctic Front

Canada is famous for its weather or, more properly, its bad weather. It is a bit of a harsh rap. Images of Scandinavia tend to turn their winters into a time of bucolic frolicking in the snow, of cross-country skiing, sleigh rides and saunas. Canadian winters —largely due to the efforts of advertisers to sell vacation trips, snow tires, auto services and the like—are portrayed as bitter, vicious and storm-filled. The reality is a mixture of both. With the exception of Vancouver and Victoria, Canadian cities endure fairly difficult winters. Montreal is reported to have more snow each year than any other major city in the world. Major blizzards hit Toronto and eastern Canada with some regularity, usually in the December to March period. The thermometer drops further on the prairies and up north; Winnipeg's blustery street corner at Portage and Main was long described as the coldest place in Canada (you can now cross the street underground). Temperatures in the minus twenties are fairly common on the prairies and can become as cold as –40°C for weeks at a time.

The winter picture is not all-dreary. Most winter days in Canada are quite pleasant—cold, perhaps, but not bitterly cold. There is a reason Canada produces so many great hockey players! Snow-covered hills make for wonderful outdoor recreational opportunities and great winter festivals, including Quebec's magnificent Carnival. Winter cold rarely holds the Maritimes in its grip for very long; the region experiences warm periods that regularly melts the snow. The most intriguing climate patterns are in Calgary and Whitehorse, where occasional bursts of warm air create "chinook" conditions, which see the temperature rise dramatically in a few hours. Vancouver and Victoria, which are snow-free for most of the winter, react poorly to the occasional storm and city traffic usually shuts down quickly. As well, Canadian urban architecture has adapted to the realities of winter. Large indoor shopping malls are common across the country, cities like Calgary and Winnipeg have an extensive corridor system linking the major buildings in the downtown core, and Toronto, Vancouver and Montreal have large underground shopping areas. Take advice on proper clothing for the weather; inadequate preparation can make life very uncomfortable. Take particular care when you are driving on winter roads, and be sure that the car is properly equipped (snow tires, chains, shovel, and other safety equipment).

Canadian Weather

As a consequence of the country's size and diversity, weather changes dramatically from coast to coast. It is not uncommon in January to find that Halifax, Nova Scotia is recording 5° C, Toronto is digging out from a massive blizzard, Saskatoon is experiencing the bitter cold of an Arctic front (with temperatures to –25° C or colder), and Vancouverites are playing tennis in a mild 12° C. The southwest corner of British Columbia (Vancouver and Victoria) has the country's most salubrious climate, noted more for rain than snow. The Maritimes (Nova Scotia, New Brunswick and Prince Edward Island) are colder than the west coast but have less snow than much of the country. Newfoundland is famous for its blustery, icy winter days. Children in St. John's often draw snow and rain coming horizontally—so strong are the winds off the North Atlantic. Even the cold regions—the prairies, central Canada and the North—enjoy warm, even hot, summers. Toronto and Ottawa suffer through hot, humid weather in July and August, and the dry heat of Manitoba and Saskatchewan can easily reach into the high 30s° C. It makes sense, then, to discover that the weather is a favorite topic of conversation for Canadians.

While Canadians adapt well to the cold winters—they plug

in their cars in the evening, bundle up in parkas, mitts and toques, and build cities and universities to permit people to stay indoors for much of the day—the country has not embraced the season. Scandinavians, with their saunas, cross-country skiing, and red-cheeked enthusiasm for a crisp winter day, have done far better at adapting to the vagaries of winter than Canadians, who seem determined to beat it back through clothing, central heating, and frequent trips to the south. Despite the country's vast northern land mass—the midpoint in Canada measured north to south is close to Yellowknife in the Northwest Territories—most Canadians actually live south of the 49th parallel. Vancouver, Montreal, Calgary, Winnipeg, Regina, Windsor, Hamilton and Toronto are located within a very short distance of the United States. The mid-North, historically the source of the nation's prosperity, has only a small percentage of the total population. Only two major cities—Saskatoon and Edmonton—are located a significant distance north of the border, and in both cases these communities are the center of a large agricultural region. Most of Canada remains northern, cold in winter, and largely unpopulated. As a further irony, tourist traffic into the far north, particularly the Yukon, Nunavut and the Northwest Territories, is largely US, European and Asian. Canadians spend far more time and money visiting Florida, Hawaii, Cuba, Mexico and other warm places than they do traveling to the northern reaches of their nation.

Conquering Distance

Vast distances have forced the country to be innovative, particularly with regards to transportation and communication. The first major national initiative was the construction of a transcontinental railway. And although the Canadian Pacific Railway project was plagued with scandals—it toppled the government of the country's first Prime Minister, John A. Macdonald—it helped unite the country politically and give a huge boost to the economy. After World War II, the effort shifted to the construction of a better road system, highlighted by the development of the TransCanada Highway in the 1950s and 1960s and the Roads to Resource program, designed to provide the developers with access to the resources in the far north. The country's road system is now first-rate, with some regional variations. Passenger rail travel, conversely, has largely disappeared, save for a network of services in Southern Ontario. Freight trains continue to play a critical role in the country's economy, and a difficult process of mergers and restructuring in the 1980s and 1990s resulted in more efficient and profitable services. Again, the country's size made Canada a leader in air travel, with bush pilots pioneering the development of air services across the country and into the far North. The small national market and government caution, however, has slowed competition. In 1999–2000, a series of bitter battles between the two largest carriers, Air Canada and Canadian Airlines International, resulted in the Montreal-based Air Canada defeating its Calgary-based competitor and forcing an airline merger which, to date, has failed to impress the traveling public. Small regional competitors, led by Westjet, have struggled to fill the void, but the supremacy of Air Canada appears to be assured, unless the government allows foreign competitors into the domestic market.

The young country invested, as well, in telegraph systems, using developing technologies to bind the country together. (Perhaps it is not surprising, therefore, that the inventor of the telephone, Alexander Graham Bell, was a Canadian and that some of the first experiments in trans-Atlantic communication took place, in part, in Newfoundland.) The country now enjoys a superb and modern communications system. It pioneered satellite television and telecommunications services, focusing on reaching people in the far northern reaches of the country. Deregulation sparked intense competition in both the land line and cellular phone sectors, with the result being the emergence of a highly competitive and sophisticated telephone industry. Canadian firms

Snowbirds

Each year, the onset of winter launches a southward migration. When birds travel south in great flocks, large numbers of Canadians are not far behind. The Snowbird phenomenon has become a significant cultural and economic force in Canadian life. The southward migration includes a diverse group: wealthy Canadians heading to private estates, middle class Canadians going south for an extended vacation, retirees who only return north long enough to protect their health insurance benefits before returning south to warmer climates, farmers who have harvested the year's crops and are waiting for planting season, and thousands of mobile home owners who try to beat the snows and head for the trailer parks in Nevada, New Mexico, Texas, South Carolina, Arizona, California and Florida. They are looking for warm weather, golf, beaches, and an escape from Canada's winter. Several million Canadians spend more than a month each year in the US, Mexico, or the Caribbean (and smaller numbers head further afield). The Snowbirds now constitute a significant market of their own, and numerous businesses have grown up to serve them (including health insurance, real estate firms, relocation services, home maintenance companies, travel agencies, and news services. One central Canadian company established an air ambulance service, which flies to the southern United States to pick up Snowbirds confined to hospitals. American medical charges are so high that provincial health authorities cover the air ambulance charge in order to get the person back into a Canadian hospital.) The lost personal spending and investment capital—now tied up in Florida condos, Mexican timeshares or trailer pads in Arizona—carries a significant cost to the Canadian economy.

have been at the forefront of the information technology revolution and, through such companies as Nortel and JDS Uniphase, have played a critical role in the expansion of the Internet. The Canadian internet backbone is among the most impressive in the world, laying the foundation for active and continued participation in the "New Economy."

The Internet Backbone

Officials in Canada, as in other countries, highlight the importance of the Internet and urge companies and citizens to get "wired." As the Internet expands around the world, it has a significant Canadian component within it. Nortel Networks is the best-known Canadian company in the Internet field, with revenues running well in excess of C$20 billion and with its operations expanding dramatically throughout the world. The company provides cutting edge products in telephone communications, data transmission, and wireless solutions. Among the firm's many products are innovative solutions in fiber-optic transmissions, switches and routers, packet telephony, modems, and various high speed data solutions. Its technical contributions to networking are widely admired and highly profitable. JDS Uniphase, another leading Canadian contributor to the Internet revolution, specializes in fiber-optics systems and provides crucial technology for telecommunications and cable television industry and also works in such areas as lasers, instrumentation, and network switches. The Ontario company has expanded dramatically in recent years and has significant markets outside of Canada.

While transportation and communication systems have both helped conquer distance and propelled the country onto the national stage, the rest of the economy has been somewhat less impressive. Few Canadian companies have truly international reputations (and those that do, like Nortel, tend to market themselves around the world as US firms). Bombardier, a maker of transportation equipment, has emerged as a major international player, but it is one of the few exceptions. Canadian business has, since the early years of Confederation, done a reasonably good job of meeting national needs, but has been less successful at bursting into the global marketplace. Many of Canada's key exports, in the automobile sector, for example, come from foreign-owned companies who use Canada as a platform for their factories and capitalize on the Free Trade Agreement (and its predecessor in this sector, the Auto-Pact) to gain access to the US market. The exception to this, of course, is Canadian resources. Canadian wheat, timber, minerals, fish and meat have found, and continue to find, significant global markets.

Skidoos to Rapid Trains

During World War II, Joseph-Armand Bombardier invented a strange-looking machine that propelled itself across the snow. Refinements turned this early prototype into the widely-used snowmobile and Bombardier dominated the marketplace. Bombardier steadily expanded its operations into other fields, and it now produces the Canadair Regional Jet, Learjet, and other business aircraft. It also produces the Sea-Doo (a recreational water sports craft) and jet boats. Bombardier has become a world leader in urban transit, and has sold trains for use in the Euro Tunnel and is currently developing the first-ever high speed train in North America. Bombardier has over 45,000 employees around the world and has annual revenues of over C$8 billion per year. Canada has long been an innovative nation in transportation technologies; Bombardier is the country's leading transportation firm and has a well-deserved international reputation for high quality, reliable and cost-effective transportation equipment.

The Canadian Welfare State

What Canada has done economically is to seek for a blend of capitalist opportunity and social welfare. Beginning in the 1940s and accelerating through to the 1970s, the federal and provincial governments have endeavoured to build a sustainable social safety net. This includes a health care system, unemployment and welfare payments, and a variety of programs aimed at personal and regional economic development. To pay for such measures, the government has maintained a comparatively high tax regime, while remaining openly committed to the capitalist economy. The system has not worked exactly as planned; the expansions of the 1960s could not be sustained through the downturn in the 1970s. And, in recent years, the government has been forced to battle a surging debt and deficit, and has accepted the prevailing international economic orthodoxy that less government is better for the country. As a result, the safety net in Canada has eroded significantly over the past decade, although state-funded and organized protections remain significantly ahead of those available in the US or Japan.

Canada developed into, as a consequence of its economic and political agenda, a comfortable middle-class nation. Until recently, organized labor was powerful and resource sector workers enjoyed significant personal incomes (the power of unions has declined and so have the wages in these sectors). At present, the strongest Canadian unions are in the bustling and profitable automotive sector and the vast Canadian public service. In general, however, Canadian workers make reasonable wages, and white and blue collar, public and private sector workers alike enjoy decent middle-class incomes. There are significant regional differences. Newfoundland and the Maritime provinces are not as wealthy as Ontario, Alberta and British Columbia. Quebec has pockets of prosperity and some sizable poor districts as well. Overriding the economic realities is the long-standing but weakening Canadian consensus that government should redistribute income, between regions and between individuals. Protective measures, such as a worker and employer-funded unemployment system, provincially-managed welfare systems, numerous wage support and retraining programs, and federal initiatives to assist disadvantaged regions help moderate the extremes of income. Wealthier Canadians are taxed at a high rate, much higher than in the US and, indeed, many industrial nations; lower income Canadians, as a consequence, benefit from decent and free (or, at least, very inexpensive) health care, subsidized post-secondary education, and an array of government initiatives aimed at children and families.

Ethnicity in Canada

The country's cultural and ethnic diversity cuts across income lines as well. While new immigrants tend to inhabit the lower reaches of the income scales, the prospects for economic progress are quite substantial. Japanese and Chinese Canadians, for example, have done very well over the past fifty years and many are among the country's wealthier citizens. New immigrants, coming from East Asia, South Asia, the Caribbean, South and Central America and Africa, typically struggle economically in the early years—and often for a generation or longer. They tend, as well, to seek out other Canadians from their former country or region and occupy cultural enclaves in the major cities. Toronto, for example, has very large Italian, Caribbean, Greek and Chinese populations. Vancouver has a very large Asian sector, dominated by Chinese (Hong Kong, Taiwan and mainland China) and East Indians, and many of these people live in ethnic neighborhoods. Small town Canada, in contrast, tends to remain largely European, although most settlements have attracted at least a few recent immigrants.

The ethnic composition of the country continues to change. Before World War II, large numbers of migrants arrived from eastern Europe, adding to the northern European population (largely British and French) that dominated the country. After World War II, the source of immigrants shifted to the south—to Italy and Greece—and the cultural diversification continued. Asian immigration, which started in the late nineteenth century, accelerated after the removal of racially-based regulations in the 1960s, and was further sparked by political unrest and, in the late 1990s, by uncertainty surrounding the Chinese takeover of Hong Kong. Canada made a concerted effort, as well, to attract wealthier immigrants, promising a place at the head of the queue to anyone willing to bring a substantial amount of investment capital into the country. Many Hong Kong residents took advantage of the opportunity to secure a Canadian passport—and therefore some security for themselves and their family—resulting in an influx of

Asian money into Canada, particularly Vancouver and Toronto. The country, which has lost many talented people to the United States over the years, has also attracted numerous professionals (doctors, engineers, technicians) from other nations; South African doctors, for example, have been attracted in large numbers to fill vacant positions in small-town Canada. While there has been some backlash against the pattern of immigration, it has been surprisingly muted—and limited to areas that, ironically, are not attracting a large number of Asian, African and Caribbean migrants.

Contemporary Challenges

While most Canadians are, in comparative international terms, doing rather well, the country is not without its compelling social issues. Urban poverty remains a key problem. Each of the major cities serves as a magnet for the dispossessed, unemployed and homeless, and local governments struggle to cope with the challenges presented by sizable populations of poor street people. That these citizens live alongside some of the richest Canadians, and often sleep in the shadows cast by the offices of leading corporations, only highlights the intensity of the issue. New immigrants, particularly those from the developing world, often struggle upon entering Canada. Those without English or French language skills face difficult adjustments. And while they can often find solace in small ethnic enclaves, their economic and social prospects are seriously curtailed. These same individuals often have little education and training; many are refugees fleeing persecution in their homeland who fled with little preparation and no money. Canadian programs provide social assistance and training, but these people typically experience difficulty moving into the economic mainstream. In some cities, notably Toronto and Vancouver, new immigrants have clashed with police, largely resulting from conflicts involving street and ethnic gangs. And while the challenges of urban violence and unrest pale in comparison to those associated with the US, the social and economic conditions of new immigrants represent a problem for Canadian authorities.

The difficulties facing aboriginal Canadians attract even more attention. First Nations (also called Indians), Inuit and Metis people have been fighting for greater recognition of treaty and aboriginal rights. While they have achieved some success before the courts, and have won some major legal victories, their communities remain economically disadvantaged. Intense social problems, including the loss of language skills and cultural traditions, bedevil the aboriginal settlements, as does widespread discrimination and the legacies of generations of racism and government domination. Aboriginal protests continue to expand. Roadblocks, generally over resource rights, have become quite common, as have occupations of government offices and organized public rallies. Non-aboriginal sympathy, however, appears to be declining, and resistance is increasing to the idea of recognizing further indigenous rights and claims. Many First Nations communities live in Third World conditions, with poor housing, shockingly high levels of unemployment, and intense internal tensions and difficulties.

That politicians have not found a solution to the First Nations issues is symptomatic of another serious national political issue: declining interest and confidence in the political process. Mirroring experiences in the United States, political participation has fallen in recent elections, and the quality of debate has worsened as well. The 1988 election, at least, included a bitter battle between the Progressive Conservative government and the Liberal and New Democratic Party (social democratic) over free trade. Subsequent elections, all won by the folksy but unimaginative Liberal leader Jean Chrétien, shied away from many policy issues and focused instead on matters of personality and regional brokerage politics (which, in turn, highlighted competition between the parties to promise the regions extra money if the party won their support). The falling quality of national and provincial politics has gone hand in glove with the global retreat from interventionist nation states and has, if anything, convinced Canadians that governments are indeed powerless to arrest the forces of economic and social globalization. At a time of dramatic national change, therefore, the country appears to be quite rudderless (save for the efforts of Finance Minister Paul Martin to constrain his otherwise free-spending cabinet colleagues and to thereby maintain healthy national surpluses at the turn of the century).

Questions About the Canadian Economy

While these other issues are important, it is Canada's economic performance that generates the greater debate and concern. Under Paul Martin's leadership, the federal government did wrestle the deficit to the ground—although the credit rests more with increased taxes and the unexpected burst of prosperity in the United States and the spill-over effect in Canada than with any dramatic cost-cutting measures by Parliament. On the surface, Canada's economy has done reasonably well. The bellwether southern Ontario industrial economy is doing exceptionally well, enjoying an economic boom that mirrors a similar expansion in the 1980s. Alberta's energy-driven expansion has produced large provincial surpluses and the prospect of a reduction, if not elimination of the provincial income tax. Canadians exports are strong, the national debt (running at a staggering C$500 billion) is slowly being paid down, and unemployment slips slowly downward. That is the good news.

The flip side of the equation is more worrisome. The Canadian dollar sits, as of December 2000, at around 65 cents to the US dollar, a sharp fall from the parity of the early 1970s. Canada's standard of living has fallen dramatically relative to the United States—by perhaps as much as 25% in the last decade. In all areas—growth rates, investment, international trade, unemployment, and the like—the United States leads Canada, sometimes by a dramatic margin. Moreover, Canada remains deeply wedded to the US economy, sending over 85% of all exports to this single, albeit impressive market. Despite much rhetoric to the country, Canada is not a significant international trading nation and retains its status as a branch plant operation of the US economy. After a flurry of economic nationalism in the 1960s and 1970s, Canadians relaxed their concern about foreign domination and have allowed non-Canadians to buy up significant portions of the country's resource and industrial producers. In the process, of course, the country has lost a substantial measure of control over its economic future.

The list of economic woes continues. Regional inequality remains as entrenched now as it was thirty years ago, despite three decades of expensive and questionable federal regional economic development programs. Cape Breton Island in Nova Scotia struggles economically, and a long-subsidized coal and steel industry is in the process of being shut down. New Brunswick's economy stumbles along, despite major provincial efforts to increase competitiveness. Prince Edward Island remains locked within an economy of agriculture and tourism, and neither holds much long-term promise. Newfoundland's fishing industry continues to founder and the prosperity introduced by the oil and gas industry is not widely shared. Outside of the main urban corridors in Ontario and Quebec, which are enjoying notable success, the small towns and resource districts of central Canada are struggling, as is much of Manitoba and rural Saskatchewan. Alberta bustles and prospers, much to the chagrin of other Canadians, who increasingly resent the province's resource wealth. British Columbia used to lead the country in economic performance and is blessed with enormous resources and great potential in Asia. Over the past decade, however, it has been saddled with a particularly inept provincial government that has flopped from scandal to misdeed, from ill-advised economic policy to favors to electoral friends. Regional equality remains one of the most important economic issues in the country, but there are few signs that regional or national politicians have any solutions at hand as to how to deal with the issue.

Canada, like other industrial nations, is feeling the increasing power of economic globalization. Its resource sectors faltered under international competition, as it finds itself losing key markets to new rivals. While the automotive sector seems secure, buttressed by ready access to the US market and the long-term protection imbedded in the Free Trade Agreement, the rest of the country's industry faces a more questionable future. There are some very successful companies, like Nortel and Bombardier, which compete well on a global scale—and which bring thousands of jobs into the country through overseas contracts. But most Canadian firms have little presence outside Canada and the United States and appear ill-prepared to take the next step into global competitiveness. At the same time, global pressures on government to lower taxes, allow greater free trade, and otherwise liberalize the national economy have been quite effective. The federal government, after years of raising taxes, has begun to back off significantly, as have provincial authorities. As a consequence, Canada is experiencing the kind of bipolar income distribution— a small but wealthy group of people at the top of the income scale, a declining middle class and a larger number of citizens in the lower income brackets—that has become the hallmark of globalization. The toner parts of Vancouver, Toronto, Calgary, Edmonton and Montreal are truly world-class in quality and character, but many other parts of the country are experiencing sharp declines in income and standard of living.

After World War II, Canada and other industrial nations developed economies based on high wage resource and industrial labor. Many of these workers have few if any major skills, but strong trade unions and general prosperity ensured that companies paid top dollar to attract and retain a reliable work force. This system served the west very well, for blue and white collar workers alike earned reasonable incomes, aspired to home ownership and contributed to a consumption-driven economy. That structure, in Canada and other countries, is eroding quickly. Global competition—whereby Canadian producers are competing with Indonesia and Russian companies—has undercut the viability of the postwar industrial model. Companies have retrenched and restructured, adding technology, shedding workers and often moving their production outside the country. Add to this the imperatives of the information economy—whereby a premium is paid for advanced skill and knowledge and where work is increasingly displaced by either computers or international competition—and the economic foundations of a country like Canada take a sharp turn for the worse. Those with marketable skills and specialized knowledge do extremely well in such an economy; those who prospered for many years with limited technical skill and no specialized knowledge are increasingly finding themselves unemployed or forced to accept dramatic wage cuts. Resolving the imperatives of the new global economy will remain one of Canada's foremost challenges.

Canadians have good reasons, in the final analysis, for worrying about the positive re-enforcement of the UN Human Development Index ranking. Much as it is a welcome honor, it speaks more to Canada's past and present condition than it does to its future. In the 1960s, Canada was one of the wealthiest nations in the world (in per capita income); it is now around eighteenth and appears destined to fall further in the coming years. The world is becoming more economically globalized, Canada more continental. At a time when dramatic and authoritative national leadership is required, the country's political leaders offer intense partisanship and a defense of the status quo.

Canada is not doomed to any immediate collapse. In fact, the country has many promising and positive attributes: a strong education system, a multicultural workforce, excellent national infrastructure, openness to international investment and business, political stability, access to the US market, bountiful resources, a strong work ethic, and a gentleness of national spirit. Visitors will find Canada to be a delightful, promising and engaging nation.

CHAPTER 2

Regional Economies, Regional Realities

Canada is a very difficult country to figure out. Regional and ethnic identities often mean far more than an over-reaching attachment to the nation. It is not that citizens are not Canadians or are not proud of their country. Rather, Canada is a very undemanding nation that requires very little, emotionally or practically, of its residents. As a Canadian historian said some thirty years ago, Canada is a country of "limited identities," with people demonstrating far more attachment to region, social class, religion or ethnicity than to the vague notions of nationalism. This carries over very strongly to the commercial world. Canada presents to the world at least seven different regional economies, with several exhibiting strong divisions internally. Much as Japan's Okinawa differs dramatically from the Tokyo district, northern England looks little like London and Arkansas bears scant resemblance to California, Canada's regions each have unique and positive characteristics that are important for international business people to understand. (A latter discussion will discuss how regionalism affects the Canadian business culture; the focus here is on broad economic issues.)

Atlantic Canada

The four eastern provinces are the poorest in Canada, and carry the burdens of history, geography and politics. Newfoundland and the three Maritime provinces, Nova Scotia, New Brunswick and Prince Edward Island, were all reluctant entrants into Confederation, fearing that union with Ontario and Quebec would result in a loss of autonomy and potential economic dislocations.

Their worst fears were realized. Once the most prosperous part of the Dominion of Canada, the Maritimes entered a prolonged recession late in the nineteenth century and have recovered only partially over time. Newfoundland resisted Canada's overtures, only to find itself in deep economic distress in the 1930s. After World War II, Newfoundland accepted Canada's offer and became the tenth province, receiving access to Canadian transfer payments and social service but surrendering its vaunted independence. Resentment still lingers on "The Rock," even though thousands of Newfoundlanders have left the island for jobs in southern Ontario and Alberta.

Building an Eastern Economy

The Atlantic provinces continue to lag behind the rest of the country in terms of employment, new business development and standard of living. Many people in the region were dismayed in recent years when Irish pubs and Maine fast-food restaurants turned to Newfoundland and New Brunswick respectively to find much-needed workers. That residents were willing to consider such options provided proof of the limited opportunities in the region. The federal government established the Atlantic Canada Opportunities Agency (ACOA) with a specific mandate of expanding economic activity in the region, using federal training and investment funds to spark private sector and public-private ventures. ACOA has a wide-ranging mandate to work with provincial and municipal governments, private business, educational institutions and other participants in the regional economy in order to create additional industrial and commercial activity and, thereby, to raise regional incomes and lower the Atlantic unemployment rate. Much of the work is developmental and involves assisting small communities and specific areas with community economic development strategies.

ACOA also has a substantial budget (over C$300 million for 2000–2001) that is used to prime the economic pump, primarily through grants, loan guarantees and forgivable loans to private sector ventures willing to establish in economically depressed zones. The organization works very closely with communities facing the closure of a major industry or government operation, and provides funding for selected start-up companies. ACOA supports Community Business Development Corporations, provides interest-free loans to small and medium-sized enterprises, offers seed capital for young entrepreneurs and makes available venture capital funds for more speculative initiatives. The organization also sponsors workshops, provides business advice, and holds training sessions on such topics as opportunities in the "New Economy" and assistance with breaking into international markets. ACOA is also heavily involved in new initiatives, announced in 2000, designed to expand Atlantic Canada's potential in information technology and to build a more competitive regional economy. Federal initiatives, such as ACOA, have been sharply criticized in other regions of the country, but the evidence does not back the accusation that ACOA wastes money on unproductive operations. Given the difficulties with economic development in the region, ACOA actually has a strong track record of backing successful firms and of securing a reasonable return on its many investments. In fact, a study of new business start-ups measured over a five-year period found that ACOA-based companies were 2 1/2 times as likely to succeed as Atlantic firms.

The Atlantic economy rested, for years, on the bounty off the Grand Banks of Newfoundland and the world famous cod stocks that seemed to promise endless opportunity. Even still, fishing was a hard life and produced more profits for the wholesalers and fishing companies than it did prosperity for the small fishers in the outposts of Newfoundland and small villages in the Maritimes. The gradual and then sharp decline in fish stocks over the past two decades sent shockwaves throughout the region. Government officials struggled to monitor the fishery and estimates of sustainable yields proved to be wildly optimistic. By the 1990s, the cod fishery had been closed, throwing thousands of fishers and fish plant workers out of work. The collapse was most pronounced on Newfoundland, but the rest of the region felt the pain of the moratorium on the cod fishery.

Through the 1960s and 1970s, the federal government had extended the national social safety net to the region. A key feature of government involvement was the unemployment system, adapted to meet the special needs of fishers and onshore workers. The government permitted seasonal workers to gain access to many months of unemployment insurance benefits—providing some measure of income security but generating unfavorable stereotypes in the rest of the country. The collapse of the cod fishery overlapped with major revisions in the unemployment insurance regulations, making it harder for regional workers to secure benefits based on the short and intense work season in the fishery. Plant workers throughout the region, and particularly on Newfoundland and the Academic peninsula suffered greatly from the pinches of declining stocks and changing government regulations.

Awareness of the frailty of the Atlantic fishery convinced federal and provincial governments to attempt a variety of regional development schemes. The Liberal Party, in office for much of the past thirty years, benefited from the power of regional power brokers and funneled millions of dollars of investment capital into such ventures as a heavy water plant in Nova Scotia, Cape Breton's money-losing steel mill and coal mines (also in Nova Scotia), and a seemingly endless string of marginal development projects (including an ill-fated oil refinery and cucumber hothouse in Newfoundland and the Bricklen luxury automobile plant in New Brunswick). Very few of these projects provided more than transitory benefits; the region gained more from politically-driven efforts to relocate federal government offices (like the Department of Veterans' Affairs, now based in Charlottetown, Prince Edward Island) in the area.

The region has pockets of considerable wealth. "Old money" exists in some abundance in Saint John and Halifax, in particular, and a visit to St. Andrews reveals both the stately past of the region and the area's tight connections to wealthy families in the American Northeast. Scotiabank (formerly the Bank of Nova Scotia) was founded on eastern money—although it has now shifted operations to central Canada. Two of Canada's richest families—the McCains (noted for their frozen foods) and the Irvings (oil refining, forestry, and transportation)—are from the region. New Brunswick, in particular, experiences the benefits and costs of their power. These two companies dominate the provincial economy, with the Irvings controlling much of the economic future of Saint John. The Irving family has built an integrated commercial empire that reaches across the border into the Northeast United States and

The Irving Family

Led for years by patriarch K.C. Irving, the Irving family dominates business in New Brunswick and, to a lesser extent, in the Maritime region. The family's closely integrated companies control most of the gas stations in the area (and down in New England as well). They also own huge tracts of forest lands in Canada and Maine, a number of large industrial plants (including a pulp mill, the continent's largest oil refinery, saw mills and other processing facilities), shipping and trucking companies, retail stores, and media outlets. No substantial part of Canada is as much under the sway of one family or group of companies as is New Brunswick. Local opinion is divided as to the costs and benefits of this domination. The Irvings are increasingly active in local philanthropic activity and their investments in major industrial ventures underpin the entire regional economy. Critics claim that the family network of companies is so large and dominant as to make competition extremely difficult and that the prominence of the Irving empire has stifled other business developments. Internally, the Irving companies are extremely well-run, adopt cutting edge business practices, and are increasingly outward looking (although recent attempts to buy up a chain of gas stations in the northeastern United States were unsuccessful). The Irvings family holdings make them among the richest people in the world—and they remain a formidable regional influence.

incorporates everything from hardware stores, shipbuilding and shipping companies to service stations and the provincial newspapers.

Efforts to transform the regional economy continue. Newfoundland is benefiting from the development of the Hibernia offshore oil field, and the province has superb research capabilities relating to fisheries and North Atlantic oceanography. Labrador holds considerable resource promise, as shown by the rich Voisey Bay nickel deposit (the development of which the province has slowed to ensure that the area garners as large a share of the employment and investment benefits as possible) and the potential construction of additional hydroelectric capacity on the Churchill River. Still, the province's population remains far behind the national norm in income, unemployment and commercial opportunity and substantial change remains far in the future. The construction of the impressive Confederation Bridge to Prince Edward Island (bitterly contested by many locals who wished to preserve island isolation) has opened the tiny province to enhanced tourism and sparked a surge in tourist-related investment. Efforts to move beyond tourism and potato production, however, have enjoyed few successes to date.

On the mainland, Nova Scotia holds greater promise, particularly in the Halifax-Dartmouth area. The area's large university population and active government creates opportunities for considerable synergy, and the arrival of Sable Island natural gas holds the promise of a resource-driven expansion. The local fishing industry remains stable, with a rich lobster market replacing the long-critical cod fishery. Cape Breton and rural Nova Scotia, in contrast, have fewer bright spots, and the pattern of government dependency that is endemic in the region is particularly strong in these areas. The people of Cape Breton are, however, a resilient and determined bunch (the local music industry is one of its strengths) and intense cooperative efforts are underway to build high-technology opportunities in the area. New Brunswick has

Newfoundland's Shot at Prosperity

For most of the twentieth century, Newfoundland endured considerable economic hardship. While the rest of the country prospered after World War II, the province suffered through wrenching economic changes, including the collapse of the outports (small fishing villages) and the closure of the long-famous Grand Banks cod fishery due to the decimation of fish stocks. For more than two decades, Newfoundlanders have tied their hopes for prosperity to the development of the oil and gas potential of the Hibernia field, over 300 km offshore. It took years to bring the field on line, but the first full year of production took place in 1998, signaling the launch of the province's fossil fuel industry and the promise of a brighter economic future. Benefits hit the area before the first barrels of oil, as Newfoundlanders and local firms were actively involved in the construction of the Hibernia oil platform. Not all the work went to locals, as a large number of western Canadians with oil field experience were brought in to work on the project. The economic impact could be seen throughout the area, however: in greater activity in the St. John's Harbour and at the local heliport (used to ferry supplies to the platform). The company worked very hard to increase local involvement, including encouraging an expansion of relevant university courses, using local suppliers when appropriate, maintaining a sizeable management office in the Newfoundland capital, and training, attracting and retaining highly skilled workers in the long moribund local economy. The project provide a substantial revenue flow for the provincial government, raising the possibility that, in time, Newfoundland would reduce its reliance on government funding and would, potentially, join the ranks of the country's "have" provinces.

areas of strength: a reasonably strong provincial forest industry, an oil refinery, the call center industry in Saint John and an emerging high technology sector in Fredericton and Moncton. Both, however, lag behind other Canadian cities in scale, depth and investment capital, and they will struggle to keep up with the fast-moving new economy. Over the past decade, the provincial government invested heavily in information technology; New Brunswick has one of the most creative telephone and television services in North America and is probably the most heavily "wired" jurisdiction on the continent, if not the world. The development has resulted in the emergence of New Brunswick as a test-bed for information technology projects (tele-health in the region remains a strength). In both provinces, the greatest strength is a comparative stability (there are few jobs to lure people away) and an extremely dependable work force. Saint John's call center industry, for example, ranks among the best in North America, largely because of the solidity and reliability of the employees.

The federal governments, whose previous efforts at economic diversification have produced uneven results at best, remains an active player in the regional economy. Before the 2000 election—and with a sharp eye to the region's 32 seats—the government made up to C$700 million available in an Atlantic Innovation Program, designed to spark expansion of the high-technology industry. The money will certainly help, not the least by infusing the region's cash-starved universities with additional cash. Whether it will be sufficient to overcome the weight of history and geographic disadvantage is difficult to judge. For now, the Atlantic region continues to struggle. It continues to fall further behind the rest of the country, and the gap between the area and the prosperity of southern Ontario and Alberta is both pronounced and increasingly evident in government programs and general standard of living. For years, Atlantic Canadians have bemoaned the fact that their greatest export has been people (particularly the graduates from their excellent universities); this reality is likely to continue.

Flopping Fast Ferries

Government and business have long worked closely together in Canada. Along with some significant successes, however, are some striking failures. Years ago, governments poured a great deal of money into the Bricklen automobile plant in New Brunswick—to no avail. Similarly, federal and provincial money has been used to prop up longtime money losing ventures across the country, from provincially supported pulp mills in British Columbia to heavily subsidized steel plants on Cape Breton. Canada's west coast provides one of the most recent examples of good intentions gone awry. The NDP government commissioned the construction of three "fast ferries" from local shipyards. The ferries were designed to add capacity on the mainland to Vancouver Island runs and to reduce crossing times. The government hoped that the successful completion of the ferries would stabilize work at the shipyards, add industrial jobs, and establish an export industry. The PacifiCats, built at considerable cost, foundered from the beginning. Cost overruns, design faults and messy political battles turned a promising industrial venture into a fiasco. Before long, the ferries were on the block. Their speed was far from stellar and there were flaws in performance. Moreover, the project had become a political liability. The provincial government then launched an embarrassing initiative to sell the three craft—only to discover that the world market for large, fast ferries operating in protected waters is very small. By the end of 2000, there were no takers. Provincial taxpayers were still waiting to learn of the final cost. All is not lost, however. One of the companies involved with the fast ferry project began producing luxury yachts and now faces a backlog of orders.

Quebec

In the 1960s, Quebec had an externally controlled, largely working class society. Over the past forty years—and despite the political uncertainty surrounding the threat of separation and the emergence of powerful First Nations governments—Quebec has modernized and expanded its economy, to the point that it is one of the most creative in the country. The province still draws heavily on its northern resources, particularly the mines and forests of the mid-north and the enormous hydroelectric potential of the James Bay/Hudson Bay drainage. Hydroelectric power provides the provincial government with a substantial cash flow and the provincial economy with a substantial commercial advantage. Such major industries as Alcan's aluminum smelter have ignored the political unrest and continue to capitalize on globally-competitive power rates. Quebec still has a solid agricultural sector, one with deep historic roots, although it is no longer an engine of growth.

Political uncertainty, Quebecers long ago discovered, brings certain benefits, the most important of which is substantial cash transfers from the federal government (which appears determined to make it so that the province could not afford to separate). Quebec does extremely well in federal procurement and subsidy programs, and the sprinkling of federal dollars on provincial businesses, local governments and combined federal-provincial projects remains a key element of regional life. Some of these, particularly investments in the aerospace sector, appear to have paid off in substantial spin-off benefits and expanded corporate activity. Montreal, which suffered for two decades from the trauma associated with the election of the Parti Quebecois, has rebounded of late, its long fabled cultural vitality increasingly matched by an outward looking and creative business environment.

Quebec, in the unusual calculus of Canadian politics, is a "have not" province (as are all the provinces but Ontario, Alberta, British Columbia and occasionally Saskatchewan). This means that it is a net beneficiary of federal payments—and Quebec gains more from this system than other parts of the country. But its citizens are not wealthy; as a result, unemployment remains comparatively high, in part because French Canadians are less likely to migrate to other parts of the country than are, for example, Atlantic Canadians. (In the 1970s and 1980s, an aggressive federal bilingualism program attracted many French Canadians to federal jobs across the country, but this initiative has been scaled back dramatically in recent years.) Rural Quebec shares much in common with Atlantic Canada. The Gaspe region and the North Shore (east of Quebec City, along the Saint Lawrence River), in particular, have suffered through long periods of economic hardship. Prosperity is largely restricted to Montreal, Hull (across the river from Ottawa, the nation's capital) and Quebec City, and some of the larger Quebec companies are world-class in quality and competitiveness. In contrast, Sherbrooke, a once vibrant industrial center, has fallen on hard times and most of the city's factories have now closed. Quebec is showing increasing promise and has shared in some of the reflected glory of Ontario's boom, but the province faces some formidable economic challenges in the years ahead.

Ontario

For generations, Ontario has been Canada's industrial heartland and the engine of the Canadian economy. That is true once again, with the US-driven industrial boom producing a rapid economic expansion in the southern part of the province in particular. Toronto is the center of Canadian finance, investment and trade. Radiating out from the provincial capital, lies the greatest concentration of manufacturing capacity in the country. Nearby cities like Oshawa (automobiles), Hamilton (steel), and further removed industrial centers like Windsor (automobiles) and Sarnia (chemicals) generate much of the country's industrial output. Much of this output is targeted at the US market, and the flow-over benefits from the burst of US prosperity have been dramatic, indeed. There is, as well, an intriguing region surrounding the industrial belt, made up of farms, vineyards, cottage industries and a growing number of home-based professional businesses, the latter benefited from easy access to urban clients and southern Ontario's facilities.

Two Ontario cities in particular, Toronto and Ottawa, are

critical to the country's potential in the new global economy. Toronto is well-connected to the US and international economy, is home to a sizable industrial base, and has the added benefit of a remarkably diverse multicultural population. Ethnic diversity is a major Toronto strength and, uncharacteristically for western industrial cities, is widely recognized. The city's commercial world is globally connected and internationally engaged. Ottawa, fifteen years ago, was a tired and unappealing government city, dominated by a bureaucracy that provided little spark or energy to the region. That has all changed. The city has grown dramatically, but largely because of the expansion of the high-technology sector. Private business now outstrips government employment as the key to the regional economy, and the area's software and technology sectors are national leaders and international competitors. Once sleepy Ottawa has become, instead, a major contributor to the global Internet revolution. Canada's future success in this critical field depends, in large measure, on Ottawa's continued success.

Outside the Windsor-Hamilton-Toronto-Ottawa corridor, the less promising imperatives of the Canadian resource sector hold sway, with these areas facing a variety of challenges. Mines and forest companies face global competition and some have had to contend with changing environmental expectations. Northern Ontario—Sudbury and Thunder Bay—have not done as well as the rest of the province in recent years. (And frustration with the difference has often resulted in grumbles about the current political structure.) The provincial government has attempted to offset the southern boom by shifting offices to northern centers, but this has not overcome the continued difficulties in the international resource economies. Mining and forestry continue, and hope springs eternal that another major discovery will fuel major economic expansion in the region. More realistically, increased effort is being paid to the tourism industry in an attempt to balance out losses in the traditional resource economy.

Saskatchewan and Manitoba

Until Ontario's recent economic surge, the most expansive economies in the country were in the west. But neither Manitoba or Saskatchewan seemed to crack the first rank of the regional economies. These two provinces have strong, stable economies, with the prosperity blemished primarily by continued uncertainty about prairie agriculture. Since the late 1890s, western farmers have been critical to the country's overall economic performance. More recently, however, a variety of forces have combined to undercut this key sector, including global competition and low crop prices, environmental problems (including floods and droughts), international debates over government agricultural subsidies, increasing cost and efficiency of equipment, the growth of factory farms, major changes in Canadian freight rates, and attempts to anticipate world demand for new crops. Efforts have been made to diversify the agricultural economy, through greater regional processing and the expansion of hog farming in the region. For the past decade, however, farmers have been frustrated by the continued decline in profitability, limited federal interest, and growing international pressures.

There is more to these provinces' economies than agriculture. Both have substantial forestry operations and there are substantial mines in the region. Manitoba has a substantial manufacturing base—its economy is actually more akin to that of Ontario than Saskatchewan— and a small but significant finance and insurance sector. Saskatoon is the most vibrant of the cities in the area; Regina is focused largely on government services and Winnipeg is still struggling to regain its turn of the century—1900, not 2000— prominence. The agricultural economy produced, over time, a network of medium and smaller-sized communities—Dauphin, Brandon, Killarney, Virden and others in Manitoba, Yorkton, Humboldt, Moose Jaw and Swift Current in Saskatchewan. Several of these (Humboldt and Yorkton being good examples) remain the center of prosperous farming districts and belie the notion that the entire agricultural economy in the west is in desperate condition. (Make no mistake, however. Western agriculture continues to face some very serious problems.) Others, including Brandon and Battleford, have sought to diversify their economies and are working hard to attract processing and manufacturing investment; Brandon is currently expanding its hog production dramatically, adding major processing plants which promise to enhance the local economy.

Both provinces face a major challenge in integrating the aboriginal population into the economy. The incomes of First Nations and Metis people lag far behind regional averages, and indigenous communities endure staggeringly high (often 80% or more) rates of unemployment. Aboriginal leaders are struggling to overcome long-term dependency on government and are seeking new commercial opportunities; they are also encouraging their young people to secure additional education, in hopes of building up the employability of future generations. To date, there have been a few successful aboriginal businesses, but not enough to change the economic realities of the indigenous population. One bright light—albeit dimmed by a series of scandals in 2000 in Saskatchewan—have been aboriginal casinos, run under special licences from provincial governments and designed to provide work and commercial opportunities for indigenous peoples.

Where Saskatchewan and Manitoba differ substantially from the Canadian norm is in their ethnic composition (more aboriginal people and historically large concentrations of population from eastern Europe) and a collectivist approach to business. There are several large Hutterite colonies in the region (and in neighboring Alberta), with their distinct, communitarian, religious and separatist approach to social and economic involvement in the provincial order. As well, large Mennonite settlements, particularly in Manitoba, introduced the strong social conscience and impressive work ethnic of these communities into the regional mix. These ethnic contributions, combined with the harsh realities of

Wheat Pools

Prairie farmers are an interesting breed—fiercely independent, hard-working, and extremely aware of their vulnerability to transportation services and fluctuating world markets. Realizing their individual vulnerability, farmers have long known the value of collective action. Not surprisingly, therefore, the cooperative movement is extremely strong on the Canadian prairies, with the Saskatchewan, Alberta and Manitoba Wheat Pools being two of the most crucial economic organizations in the region. The Saskatchewan Wheat Pool is the largest of three, with revenues in excess of C$3 billion per year in their grain marketing and agricultural marketing cooperative. The organization does more than run grain elevators and market farm products; they have expanded their operations into value-added production, farm supplies and services, bakery supply, livestock marketing, commercial research, publishing (the *Western Producer* is read more widely than any other western Canadian newspaper) and other ventures designed to strengthen the financial position of their members. Agricore, created following a merger of the Manitoba Wheat Pool and Alberta Wheat Pool in 1998, distributes and markets grain, oilseeds and other crops and provides agricultural products for its over 83,000 members from Ontario to northeastern British Columbia. Prairie farmers have not had an easy run in recent years, largely due to substantial changes to the Canadian transportation system, sharply rising fuel and transportation costs, intense international competition, and declining government support. Farmers have been frustrated by their inability to gain greater attention and financial assistance from the federal government. As in the past, they will continue to work cooperatively through producer organizations in an attempt to moderate the financial effects of the different global market for prairie agricultural products.

pioneering life on the prairies and entrenched anger at the eastern business interests which controlled the railways and the wheat markets, produced a strong social democratic ethos and a cooperative approach to economic affairs. Prairie cooperatives—

the Manitoba Wheat Pool and the Saskatchewan Wheat Pool foremost among them—have long figured prominently in regional development. They have been harmed somewhat by the decline in the western economy and the shift from family to factory farms and are currently seeking to reinvent their operations to better suit contemporary realities.

Alberta

The Province of Alberta is on a roll. The provincial government continues to rack up impressive surpluses and has led the nation in paying down government debt. It has the lowest tax rates in the country—and no provincial sales tax (the only province without such a tax). Fifteen years ago, the provincial economy was based on agriculture and a booming oil and gas industry. The latter collapsed for a time, causing considerable hardship. More recently, Alberta offers a comprehensive and complex economy—based, in no small measure, on companies lured to the province from Ontario and British Columbia. Oil and gas has rebounded, although the approach to this sector is more realistic than in the past, and agriculture remains important. Regional centers, like Grande Prairie, Red Deer and Lethbridge draw heavily on the economic strength of farming and, in the south, ranching. Provincial tourism, based on Calgary's rustic image as a cow town, Edmonton's cultural events, and the world-class attractions of Banff and Jasper National Parks (both deep in the Rocky Mountains) is booming. Calgary is the country's most expansive and innovative urban economy and continues to attract business. Edmonton is more staid, but it too hosts some important manufacturing plants and continues to enjoy commercial success. (Edmonton is also home to the "world's largest" shopping center, the West Edmonton Mall, the only retail complex in Canada that is marketed as a tourist attraction—as befitting its hundreds of stores, hotel, entertainment complex, indoor amusement park, faux beach and wave pool.) Edmonton's main advantage is that it provides the window on northern Alberta—a resource-rich area (oil and natural gas, the Athabasca tar sands, and vast harvestable timber stands) that promises to attract continued national and international investment.

Alberta is unabashedly pro-business and has worked extremely hard to create a favorable climate for commerce. In doing so, it has run up against opposition from other interests; budget-driven cost-cutting measures in the medical, education and university sectors generated considerable protest. With the budgetary problems essentially solved, the government is starting to put more money into the public service (although much more cautiously than in the past). Government services are among the best in the country, but even here there is a willingness to experiment. The provincial government has, for example, run into federal opposition over its willingness to encourage the development of private medical clinics, in seeming defiance of the objectives of the national health system. In the past, Alberta tried too hard to spark economic development, spending vast sums of public money on diversification schemes and subsidies for incoming businesses. At times, in fact, the willingness to spend money seemed to outstrip the need to offer assistance. This open-pocket approach did not provide a solid foundation for commercial development and has been replaced, in recent times, with an emphasis on getting the basic infrastructure in place and maintaining a highly competitive tax and regulatory regime.

Other Canadians envy Alberta's success—and are often too quick to attribute their prosperity to the substantial oil and gas revenues that the province receives (see British Columbia). Alberta attracts sizable interprovincial migrations—the Athabasca tar sands development is substantially staffed by Newfoundlanders, for example—and will continue to do so. The province contributes significantly to federal transfer programs, and does so with surprisingly little complaint. The resources help, and the provincial government has attempted to stockpile revenues for future generations in the Alberta Heritage Fund. But much of Alberta's current success rests on maintaining a US-style approach to government and business and to its ability to respond quickly to new opportunities. There is every sign that the province will continue to lead the nation in economic and population growth.

British Columbia

While Alberta is the country's richest province, British Columbia probably should be. The province has all of the natural attributes any jurisdiction could hope for: vast coastal and inland timber resources, oil and gas reserves in the far northeast, massive amounts of hydroelectric power, enormous supplies of fresh water, abundant mineral deposits, and two sizable agricultural areas (the Okanagan and the Lower Fraser Valley, both blessed with gentle climates and excellent soil). It is strategically located next to the vibrant US Northwest economy; Seattle and the Microsoft-driven high-tech economy is only three hours away by car. British Columbia faces west to Asia, and its two major ports (Vancouver and Prince Rupert) offer quick and cheap access to the massive Japanese, Chinese and East Asian markets. The landscape is simply stunning, among the most beautiful in the entire world, and ranges from majestic coastal and inland mountain ranges, to dry, rolling ranchlands in the interior, surging rivers and hundreds of natural attractions that make British Columbia an easy sell to tourists. Over the years, the province has attracted a diverse population, and hosts large numbers of Chinese-Canadians, Indo-Canadians, Japanese-Canadians, Greek-Canadians, Italian-Canadians and German-Canadians, providing British Columbia with easy access to most of the major cultures and economies of the world. Add to this the most gentle climate in Canada, the quaint attractions of Victoria on Vancouver Island—famous for its British character— and the multicultural character of Vancouver, one of the world's most beautiful cities—and one has a province with unlimited economic potential.

But British Columbia continually falls short of realizing this potential. The province has lagged behind the rest of the country in economic growth in recent years, and there are sharp divisions between the strong growth of the Lower Mainland (Vancouver and environs) and the inland districts, and a much deeper division between First Nations and non-aboriginal residents. It has been plagued, other Canadians assert, with a relaxed attitude toward public policy that comes from having it too easy. Its political culture is, to put it politely, a little odd. In recent years, four premiers have had to step aside due to scandals (although, to be fair, NDP premier Mike Harcourt stepped aside to take a bullet for his party, making it possible for the NDP to regain office in the next election. His predecessor, however, was forced out in a cloud of suspicion and under the threat of criminal charges.) British Columbia has long been divided politically, with the union movement supporting the social democrats and with the other parties coalescing into a right-wing, anti-NDP coalition. It has made, over time, for colourful theater and questionable government. The province continually finds itself compared—unfavorably—to Alberta and has seen its eastern neighbor enjoy stronger economic growth for a number of years.

British Columbia's resource sector is in some difficulty. The forest sector remains critical to the provincial economy. It has, however, been harmed by labor strife, battles with government over tax rates and regulatory systems, international competition, slowness to innovate (causing the loss of some Japanese trade to Scandinavia), conflicts associated with environmental movements and aboriginal land claims, and a loss of local control through foreign investments. Logging towns have faced sharp changes in employment and even the once-stable pulp sector has endured major restructuring and layoffs. The mining sector has slowed to a crawl. Several long-operating mines reached the end of their productive lives and they and the neighboring company town were shut down. Tumbler Ridge, once the symbol of a major resource connection to Japan, is in the midst of a painful downsizing, with the town selling off homes and apartments for a fraction of their original value. Very little exploration is occurring, as mining companies worry that any mineral discoveries will immediately face environmental challenges. The provincial government's aggressive campaign to expand the provincial park system has been taken as a further sign that mining has a limited future. A long-term controversy over Alcan Aluminium Ltd's Kemano Completion Project (Alcan was, under the terms of an earlier agreement, expanding its hydroelectric capacity and the project was unilaterally canceled by the provincial government) has worried potential investors about the reliability of provincial authorities and long-term resource deals. The once strong fishing industry has been reduced dramatically in size and importance. Poor resource management, an extension of aboriginal fishing rights, and rapidly declining fish stocks have forced significant cutbacks in both the commercial and sports fishing areas. Coastal communities that once thrived on the backs of fishing and fish processing have found themselves facing increasingly difficult times.

British Columbia's tourism industry, in contrast, is booming; the province's "Super, Natural B.C." campaign has paid off handsomely. Vancouver International Airport serves hundreds of thousands of travelers each year. Eco-tourism is particularly popular, and the province's white water rafting industry has become world-famous. Even more impressively, British Columbia's skiing sector continues to expand. Huge resorts have been built near the coast (there are three ski hills overlooking Vancouver) and further in the interior, and they have attracted clients from around the world. The region's cruise ship industry, tied into the ever-popular Alaska Inside Passage cruises, remains extremely popular and counts for tens of thousands of visitors per year. Add to these the dude ranches, fishing camps, big game hunting lodges, and wilderness excursions offered in the interior, and one has the makings of a vibrant, sustainable industry.

World's Best Ski-Hills

Over the past twenty years, Canadian ski-hills have emerged as the most impressive skiing operations in the world. The Whistler/ Blackcomb area north of Vancouver is generally regarded to be the best ski resort available around, offering challenging, safe and reliable skiing (including helicopter skiing for the adventurous), superb lodges and hotels, fine-dining and all the services one would expect in a world-class facility. Massive private investment in the area has seen a steady expansion of the skiing facilities, improvements to the access highway, and the growth of rental accommodations, condominiums and services. Whistler/ Blackcomb are among the most aggressive marketers in Canada, and are very successful at keeping their resorts in the skiing public's eye (and in broadening out the season through the construction of summer attractions, like top-notch golf courses). *Conde Nast Traveller Magazine*, a discerning guide for wealthy vacationers, ranked three Whistler/Blackcomb resorts as the top in the world in 2000. The British *Daily Telegraph* agreed with the first-place ranking of Whistler/Blackcomb, incidentally, placing Banff, Alberta in second spot. The commercial consequences of the promotional success and the quality of the skiing resorts have been notable, including a steady rise in regional tourism and the development of hundreds of skiing related businesses in British Columbia.

British Columbia has other commercial strengths, although business continues to complain about the lack of political stability, wage and tax rates, and the comparatively high costs of doing business in the province (particularly in Vancouver). The province's high technology sector has shown signs of great promise, and the attractive lifestyle of the Lower Mainland has helped the area attract the highly sought after workers. The most successful area in recent years has been the ability to attract foreign, particularly Chinese, investment. In the years surrounding the Chinese takeover of Hong Kong, Vancouver became home to thousands of new Chinese immigrants, many of them bringing large amounts

Cruise Industry

The west coast of North America—rugged, mountainous, and wonderfully scenic— is home to an extremely active cruise ship industry. The standard route, which runs for 14 days, starts in Vancouver, British Columbia, and works its way up the Inside Passage, to the Alaska Panhandle and the old-time ports of Ketchikan, Juneau and Skagway. Over 300 ships per year leave from Canada Place—one of the most majestic public facilities in the country—or the nearby Ballantyne Pier, carrying almost one million passengers in total. Such companies include Holland American, Royal Caribbean, Crystal Cruises, Japan Cruise Line, Radisson Seven Seas, and Mitsui OSK Line. Estimates suggest that cruise ship passengers spend over C$300 million in the city each year, providing traffic for the airport and filling the city's hotels throughout the cruise season.

The Canadian tourism industry continues to grow. Vancouver-based cruise ships ply the Inside Passage from southern British Columbia to the Alaskan panhandle and serve tens of thousands of passengers a year through exquisite facilities on Burrard Inlet.

of investment capital. Housing and land prices were pushed up by the new money, but the immigrants brought much-needed vibrancy to the local economy. These same investors have lost interest in recent years, as returns on British Columbian operations have slipped relative to Alberta or Washington State.

For too long, however, British Columbia rested on its laurels, specifically its resource wealth, natural beauty and enthusiastic immigrant population, and did not do enough to stimulate local economic development. Grand schemes—the province has long been famous for mega-projects—mostly fell by the wayside and few of them returned the promised benefits. In fact, the failure to undertake some critical projects (improvements to the Vancouver road system, a possible bridge to Vancouver Island, and major investments in the interior and North) has slowed growth and limited inland opportunities. Northern British Columbia, for example, has long counted on its abundant resources to produce jobs and corporate profits. Increased competition and company difficulties have harmed local development. Even the construction of a new university in Prince George has not been enough to offset the downscaling of the northern resource economy.

British Columbia continues to frustrate its promoters and to fall short of its economic and social potential. Sharp social divisions—of class, ethnicity and location—continue to plague the province and are strongly reflected in its political life. The province tends to oscillate between parties of the extreme right and extreme left, and it retains (somewhat unfairly) a reputation for labor radicalism (which is now focused primarily in the public sector). British Columbia has not fully yet capitalized on its resource wealth, multicultural population, profitable location and physical beauty. There is, however, still no sign that the province has either the consensus or sense of urgency required to push the region forward in the way that Alberta has done and continues to do.

Northern Canada

Most of Canada is located in the sub-Arctic and Arctic. Three territories—the Yukon, Northwest Territories and Nunavut—collectively represent over 50% of the land mass of the country. They are, however, home to many more caribou than human beings. The population of the Yukon and Northwest Territories together is that of a small southern town, and Nunavut has only a tiny number of people in a vast district. The people that live in the North are widely scattered. In the Yukon, most of the population is in Whitehorse, the capital city, and Yellowknife holds close to 50% of the population of the Northwest Territories. Most of the communities in the territorial north are villages and hamlets; only a few have more than 2,000 residents. Costs are extremely high, as food and supplies are either brought in by barge or, more expensively, flown in. Government is by far and away the most important economic sector, with the north receiving per capita subsidies that are much higher than even the most dependant parts of southern Canada.

The northern economy has, in its day, attracted enormous interest. Furs and whalers drew traders into the region in the eighteenth and nineteenth centuries. The Klondike Gold Rush in the Yukon in 1896-1900 touched off a stampede that brought tens of thousands of cheechakos (newcomers) into the far northwest (most of them left almost as soon as they arrived, when they discovered that the gold-bearing ground had already been staked). The prospect of major oil fields first drew prospectors to the Mackenzie valley in the 1920s, and brought them back in large numbers in the 1970s. Explorations pushed into the Beaufort Sea and the Arctic Islands; significant deposits were identified, but the cost of bringing the supplies to market have, to this point, slowed many of the major developments (an oil pipeline does connect the Norman Wells area, discovered in the 1920s, with the Alberta grid). There have been other discoveries, particularly during the resource boom of the 1950s and 1960s, when mines opened across the territorial north, but by the 1990s, most were closed and the mining economy had declined dramatically.

Tourism provides one spark of optimism. Japanese tourists, in particular, are attracted by opportunities to view the Northern Lights. Germans love the wilderness of the Yukon—and, in the summer months, there are direct weekly flights from Germany to Whitehorse! Wilderness adventurers find much that is compelling: world class hunting and fishing opportunities, whitewater rafting excursions, challenging canoeing expeditions, mountain climbing (particularly in the St. Elias Mountain Range in the southwest Yukon), wildlife viewing, and cultural encounters with the region's indigenous population. There are even cruise ships venturing into the frigid and mysterious waters of the high Arctic islands. Majestic scenery, abundant wildlife, and wide open, largely undeveloped spaces resonate well with residents of crowded urban environments—particularly during the warm summers, when the sun shines for almost 24 hours a day and when there is little risk of adverse conditions. The long winters, are another thing. The Yukon has had some success marketing skiing, dog-sledding and winter festivals, and Northern Lights viewing seems to be building a clientele. But these are small, niche markets, with only limited growth potential.

Canada's northern territories face an uncertain economic future. Current levels of prosperity—the non-aboriginal population in the region does quite well, but the indigenous people have many fewer prospects—are sustainable only with continued government support. There is no certainty that the high level of federal subsidies will continue. Government is business in the North, and the subsidy culture underpins a great deal of commercial activity in the region. Territorial governments are anxious to develop new markets and new employment opportunities. There are lots of proposals on the table, but few of them hold much promise. What is more, even resource developments are returning fewer economic benefits to the region. In the 1960s, major mines revolved around a quickly built company town, which shut down when the mine closed. At present, most mining companies operate on a fly in, fly-out base, housing their staff (except locally-hired aboriginal workers) in trailers and rotating them back to southern cities on a regular basis. This system lessens social disruptions and makes it easier to open and close mines as market and resources dictates, but it also means that the major benefits from mineral developments go outside the territorial north.

Canada is, of course, more than the sum of its parts. Many Canadian firms draw on resources, people, and operations from different regions of the country. The major financial institutions serve the entire country, as do the main news outlets (the Canadian Broadcasting Corporation's radio and television service and the two national newspapers, *The Globe and Mail* and the *National Post*). To the world, the regional diversity of Canada is masked by general impressions about vast wilderness, cold winters, international decency, and a high national standard of living. Inside the country, however, regionalism matters. The various provinces and regions have vastly different economies and approach commercial development in unique ways. Strategies vary from dependency on government (Territorial North and, less dramatically, Atlantic Canada), government-led economic development (Atlantic Canada, Manitoba and Quebec), inconsistency (British Columbia), getting the economic fundamental rights (Ontario and Alberta), and cooperation and community energy (Saskatchewan). Each area can claim its share of success and failures, but some regions are clearly doing better than others. Ontario, Alberta, Saskatchewan, Quebec and Manitoba, in roughly that order, provide the most responsive business environments. Atlantic Canada and British Columbia are rather more complex to approach, for vastly different reasons. And, in time-honored Canadian fashion, the order could easily turn around very dramatically. (In the early 1990s, British Columbia had the "open for business" shingle out prominently and Ontario was wrestling with a quirky NDP government that found itself in a deep fiscal mess. Likewise, New Brunswick's government through the 1990s was the most aggressive high technology jurisdiction in the country, while Quebec was preoccupied with nationalist politics.) When political problems are added to geographical and cultural differences, it becomes evident that business people had best understand Canada's regional variations.

CHAPTER 3

The Canadian
Business Environment

Canada has a great deal to offer foreign business people—far more than proximity to the United States and ease of access due to the North US Free Trade Zone. It has a vibrant free market economy, enormous resources, a diverse, multicultural population, stable and respected government institutions, and a friendly and accessible business environment. It may not, on first glance, appear as open and dynamic as the United States—image matters a lot in these matters, and US business has been getting great international press in recent years—but Canada's opportunities are formidable. Understanding the national business environment, with the usual caveats about regional diversity, will help business people better capitalize on the options before them.

Labor

Canada has a strong, stable and well-trained work-force. It is easier to find skilled workers in Canada than in most parts of the United States and wage rates tend, after currency differences are taken into account, to be lower. Canada sends a very high percentage of its high school graduates to university or college—the country generally ranks second to the United States in this category— and the post-secondary institutions provide consistently strong training. (Fluctuations in the quality of education vary little between Canadian institutions of higher learning, as government subsidies ensure consistent standards across the country. This is very different than most other countries, including the United States, where the gap between the top and bottom schools is quite dramatic.) While there are shortages in some key skilled technical areas, the country has an open immigration system that encourages the entry of people with skills in high demand. The annual infusion of some 250,000 new immigrants keeps the Canadian labor market dynamic and provides a steady stream of workers willing to tackle entry level positions. (Even here, government programs generally provide English or French language training and educational upgrading, where required; most provinces have strong support programs for companies willing to hire and train immigrants.)

With all of the obvious problems with large generalizations, it is fair to say that Canadians have a reasonably strong work ethic. It does not compare to that of the Japanese and many East Asians but competes favorably with most other western industrial nations. Canadians are, if anything, dependable workers and provide fair value for money earned. Stereotypes about Quebecois and Atlantic Canadian workers are unfair; when companies have established viable, long-term enterprises, they are generally extremely pleased with the workforce they recruit. High technology and call center companies attracted to New Brunswick and Nova Scotia have generally lauded the quality of their workers and compare them very favorably to the more transient employees that they manage in the United States. (There is an important issue here. Canadians tend to be very regional. Many prefer to remain in their province or home town and are often prepared to accept less pay or less challenging positions in order to do so. Not all stay; there is a large annual migration from eastern Canada to Ontario, Alberta and British Columbia—and a substantial reverse flow as well. The attachment to place has often proved very beneficial to companies seeking to attract and retain workers.)

Trade unions have, at different times, been very strong in Canada and the country has endured significant periods of labor-management turmoil. British Columbia, in particularly, was historically noted for clashes between workers and management. Economic difficulties in recent times have undercut the power of trade unions considerably. They are strongest in the wealthy and stable automobile sector (where the Canadian Auto Workers Union is particularly influential) and in the Canadian public sector. Unions used to be very strong in the western Canadian resource industries, particularly logging, but global competition and corporate restructuring has significantly reduced the size and authority of these unions. The public sector unions are by far the most assertive in Canada, and health care workers in particular have come in conflict with their employers (hospitals and, indirectly, the provincial government). Even here, however, there have been major changes. Canada Post, a crown corporation, was notorious for labor-management strife. The impact of competition from couriers, email and other electronic services brought the sides together and resulted in the development of a far more cooperative relationship. US competition has tended to undercut union activity and has forced many companies to outsource significant parts of their operations in order to stay in business (the central Canadian telephone sector is perhaps the best example of this process).

Multiculturalism is definitely a commercial advantage. Canada is officially bilingual (New Brunswick is the only province to match the federal commitment to English and French services) and there is a sizable supply of workers able to operate in both official languages. Most of these, incidentally, speak French at home, although the nation's massive French immersion initiative started in the 1970s is producing a growing number of high school graduates who speak both languages quite well. New Brunswick, Quebec, Ontario and Manitoba have the largest pools of bilingual workers. From Montreal west, there are also very large immigrant populations (rural Quebec and Atlantic Canada have attracted, proportionately, much fewer new Canadians and retain a strongly European cast to the population). Toronto, Winnipeg, and Vancouver, in particular, have large concentrations of foreign language speakers, many with first-hand business experience in other countries. Canadian firms have historically not utilized this

Car Cities

Canada was an early entrant into the automobile manufacturing industry, although its home-grown firms, like the McLaughlin Carriage Company, were eventually purchased by United States-based firms. Canadian factories remained active in the sector, and, after the negotiation of a critical AutoPact with the United States in the 1960s, there was a surge in sales to the United States as well. The automobile industry is the engine of southern Ontario's economy and has been largely responsible for the sustained prosperity of the region. Windsor, immediately across the river from Detroit, Michigan, is one of Canada's key industrial centres. Henry Ford invested in the city early in the twentieth century, and Chrysler, Ford and General Motors (along with hundreds of small auto-parts manufacturers) collectively employ over 30,000 workers in the area. Production of Chrysler's famous minivan and Ford's F-Series truck engines are based in Windsor. Oshawa, 50 kilometers east of Toronto, is the home of General Motors Canada and is similarly dominated by the automobile assembly and auto parts industry.

Windsor and Oshawa are known, as well, for the prominence of trade unions and have long provided strong support to the New Democratic Party. Differences over bargaining strategies and cross-border priorities convinced the Canadian branch of the United Auto Workers to break away, almost en masse, in 1984-1985. The following year, in 1986, the newly formed union was officially named the Canadian Auto Workers. It remains a formidable and important partner in the Canadian automobile and industrial economy. CAW is the largest public sector union in Canada, with its almost 240,000 members organized into 400 local unions and 1600 bargaining units. The CAW is also an outspoken proponent of Canadian economic nationalism.

talent pool very well, although Chinese Canadian entrepreneurs in British Columbia have begun to develop a large number of Asian-centered businesses which draw on the language skills and cultural knowledge of these workers. Canada has historically welcomed migrants and refugees from around the world and has large concentrations of immigrants from across Europe, Asia, Africa, the Caribbean and South America; with only a few exceptions, however, the country has not capitalized on the available expertise as much as they might.

Multicultural Commerce

Canada has a series of commercial ethnic enclaves, most offering food stores, restaurants, travel services and other facilities with a strongly ethnic flavour. Perhaps the best example of this can be found in Richmond, British Columbia, a suburb of Vancouver. Over the past twenty years, this city of 160,000, has changed dramatically from a Euro-Canadian, middle-class enclave into a multicultural community, with close to one-third of its population being of Chinese ancestry. Another 7% are South Asian and a further 3% are Filipino. While most of the cities' services and stores operate in English, several commercial districts have a decidedly Chinese character. External and internal store signs are quite often in Chinese, and there are major markets and speciality stores catering to Chinese clients. First time visitors are often perplexed by the sight of large stores and malls targeted at a single non-English speaking ethnic group—but many venture inside and are delighted at the commercial variety and cultural ambiance of these stores.

Canadian labor is definitely a national asset, and most of the trade unions are quite comfortable working with new and existing business to develop competitive, sustainable operations. (They have learned, from bitter experience, the reality of continental and global competition and are truly anxious to work with management to keep Canadian operations in place). There is considerable mobility within Canada—both from one company to another and from one region to another—itself a reflection of the economic uncertainty that plagued the country through the 1980s and 1990s and which undercut personal loyalty to firms. Companies establishing operations in Canada will generally find

Canada's ethnic minorities often congregate—at least for business purposes—in specific communities. Richmond, a suburb of Vancouver, has a large concentration of Chinese-Canadians and, as a consequence, a very active Chinese business sector.

a ready supply of able, hard-working employees, easily trained (often with government financial help) and reliable. The workers will, in global terms, be competitive and productive, and are generally open to the adoption of modern manufacturing and communication technologies.

Environmental Protection

Canada is blessed with remarkable physical resources and vast wilderness areas. It has not been as pro-active as the United States in protecting these areas from development, relying it seems on the simple scale of its undeveloped lands to protect the country's future. There has, over the years, been growing concern about airborne pollutants, and eastern Canada has paid a heavy price for the spread of acid rain from eastern US and central Canadian industrial plants. British Columbia is the nation's leader in protecting wilderness areas (over some business objections, particularly from mining interests) and the federal government has established several new national parks, particularly in northern areas. Canada is, as well, an active player in the global environmental movement, having been the home base for Greenpeace in the early years and, again in British Columbia, hosting strong and active environmentalist organizations. Canada was active in the Rio and Kyoto environmental accords and attempted to serve as a political broker between industrial and poorer nations during the follow up to the Kyoto Summit on environmental protection.

Environment concerns figure quite strongly, then, in Canadian business operations. The country's major polluting industries—pulp and paper, smelters, power stations, and the like—have been required to go through expensive retrofits to bring them in line with current environmental standards. Expectations for new industries are similarly high, and environmental assessments have become an integral part of any new resource or industrial development. Community sensitivities run very high, and there

Environment and Business in Conflict

Environmental concerns mean a lot to many Canadians, and major resource projects have, for almost forty years, attracted a great deal of attention and often public protests. Concern over potential environmental and social impacts shut down the proposed Mackenzie Valley and Alaska Highway gas pipelines before construction could begin. Forestry and hydro-electric projects in central Canada likewise attracted strong opposition, particularly by First Nations people. British Columbia is the hotbed of Canadian environmentalism and it is also a resource-rich province. Over the past decade, a series of major battles pitted developers against loose coalitions of aboriginal rights advocates and environmentalists. The Kemano Completion Project called for the construction of additional hydro-electric capacity for Alcan's aluminum smelter at Kitimat. Faced with a divided North and growing southern opposition to the project, the British Columbia government cancelled the half-built dam (an action they subsequently paid for with a negotiated settlement with Alcan). Similar conflicts over a proposed mine in the Tatshenshini area of northwest British Columbia saw the government once again side with environmental protestors. A struggle over logging in old growth forest at Clayquot Sound on Vancouver Island was more complex. Determined environmentalists chained themselves to equipment, forced the police to arrest them, and otherwise struggled to save the ancient trees. Aboriginal groups were more ambivalent this time around, for many of their community members were active in the logging industry. Government and company negotiators worked hard and long to find a sustainable and acceptable solution (environmentalists have, at times, organized effective international campaigns targeting companies which cut old growth timber). Clayquot Sound is now the focus for land claims negotiations between the First Nations and federal and provincial governments. Resources remain very important to the Canadian economy, but developers no longer have the free hand that they enjoyed in earlier decades. Environmentalists, First Nations and local residents watch proposed projects very carefully and are quick to protest if they feel that the development is not properly structured or environmentally sensitive.

are often local clashes over proposed industrial developments (with particular rancor saved for discussions of the disposal of urban or industrial wastes). Environmental lobby groups work very hard to pressure governments to toughen regulations, protect wildlife and wilderness lands, and halt major resource developments. Mining, pipeline, logging and hydroelectric projects have, in particular, been singled out for public debate. Most have proceeded, albeit with costly changes at times; several have been canceled by government or postponed by investors.

Standards

Canadian businesses are expected, as befits the nation's first world standing, to adhere to high industrial and commercial product standards. Federal and provincial governments monitor health and safety standards quite closely; the country differs dramatically from Mexico and substantially from the United States in the range and variety of commercial operations. Workplace standards are strongly enforced (and are monitored by labor unions and support groups, even in non-union situations, to ensure that workers are not exploited or put in dangerous situations). There are stringent requirements for safety gear, proper procedures and the like, and it is expected that these rules will be attended to closely.

On the product side, the Canadian government follows similar testing and assessment procedures as the United States—albeit more slowly and with much fewer resources. There is a tendency to rely on, or build off of, US testing procedures, such as those undertaken by the Federal Drug Administration in the United States. Major cutbacks in federal government scientific operations have resulted in allegations that existing standards are not being fully applied. In general, however, Canadians products are required to meet exacting health and safety standards, are subject to extensive government and consumer testing (i.e.. by consumer organizations), and therefore meet acceptable levels of reliability and safety.

Protected Markets (Marketing Boards)

Canada is not a completely open market and several key agricultural sectors enjoy the protection of government-sanctioned marketing boards, operating through such agencies as the National Farm Products Marketing Council (eggs, chickens, broilers hatching eggs and turkeys), Canadian Pork Council, National Dairy Council, Prince Edward Island Marketing Board, Ontario Wheat Producers Marketing Board, and Ontario Grape Growers Marketing Board, to highlight a few. These marketing boards are structured to protect producers from competition and to ensure the long-term viability of the industry, and typically operate on a provincial level. Ontario, for example, could buy milk much more cheaply from the United States, but the milk marketing board allocates quotes between farmers and keeps out foreign competition, thereby increasing the price to consumers and returns to the producers. This system—which operates on a much smaller basis than the massive agricultural subsidies that have historically been available in Japan, Britain and France (and even the United States)—protects Canadian suppliers, ensures the steady availability of locally-produced products, and stabilizes the farming communities and regions which provide these valuable supplies. Because of these marketing boards, related industries (such as ice cream production) have flourished in the surrounding areas, providing further economic stimulus to the agricultural economy. Canada's major agricultural exports, such as wheat, canola and beef, do not operate under the protection of domestic marketing boards.

Advertising and Promotion

Canada's advertising and promotion structure mirrors that of the United States. The two countries share television stations (more Canadians watch US stations than the reverse) and magazines. The latter were the focus of a lengthy debate in Canada, as advertisers in US magazines (even those with a Canadian edition, like *Time*) were not able to deduct these as business expenses. The goal, obviously, was to support Canada's national magazine industry—a fairly standard government procedure. That rule was recently changed, opening up US magazines, which have wide readership in Canada, to Canadian advertisers. The television situation is more unusual. Most US programs carry US advertisements. If a Canadian television station shows a program at the same time that it airs on a US station (having paid for the right to do so), Canadian advertisements appear on both versions of the program. As a consequence, Canadians see Canadian advertisements (some featuring US products) on Canadian programs, Canadian advertisements on some US programs (particularly from border-area television stations), and US advertisements on most US shows. Given the cross border markets for most consumer products, many Canadians do not notice a huge difference in the advertisements. Certain kinds of US advertisements—for the US Marines, US health care providers, US lawyers (who often offer bizarre, combative advertisements promising fast returns from legal action), and US grocery stores—generate a quick laugh in Canada, for they have no bearing on local markets.

Radio stations, in contrast, are highly localized (except the CBC, which is a national service and which does not carry advertisements). While a few of them carry US programming—including shock-radio host Howard Stern and a variety of the psychological advice programs that are unique to the United States—advertising is targeted at local audiences. (Internet radio, those available around the world, has not yet had an appreciable impact on advertising in Canada.) Many companies use radio advertisements to promote in-store events and special corporate activities; they are used less regularly for simply product promotion.

US retail chains, like The Home Depot, continue to make great headway in the Canadian market. These chains benefit from Canadian access to US television advertising and a general Canadian enthusiasm for American discount retailing.

US-styles, products and fads carry considerable cache in Canada. Even marketing trends that have little cultural resonance in Canada—like rap music and African-US urban chic—nonetheless prove popular with young people. US products not readily available in Canada—particularly in such market-sensitive areas as young women's clothing—hold special appeal, and are now readily available through Internet web-sites. Ready Canadian access to US popular culture—television, movies, music and magazines—means that young Canadians, in particular, are strongly influenced by US advertising trends and promotions and look for heavily promoted products in local stores.

Even a quick overview of Canadian and US advertising reveals some significant national differences. With the exception of used car advertisements—which seem deliberately tacky in both countries—US advertisements tend to be more aggressive and status-oriented than their Canadian counterparts. Canadian stores promote good value and prompt service; US operations suggest lifestyle improvements and family-type atmospheres in the stores. Of course, there are many stores and restaurants which operate in both countries, and these chains tend to offer the same advertisements on both sides of the border. The smaller Canadian regional markets, as well, tend to result in fairly low-cost advertisements on local television and radio stations—although their local US counterparts often reveal pretty basic production values as well. (Both, incidentally, offer abundant proof of why small furniture and retail stores should never make their own advertisements!)

Franchises and Small-Level Entrepreneurship

Canada does not have a strong entrepreneurial ethos. It exists, but is contained largely within the new immigrant communities. Immigrants run many of the small stores (corner groceries, laundries, small restaurants, shoe and clothing repair, and the like) across the country. The country does not have the strong speculative fever that infects the United States, although there is cross border interest in get-rich quick schemes (which can be seen running as paid advertisements on late night television) and personal selling systems, like Amway. Unlike Japan, China, Taiwan, or other countries, where most people seem to see themselves as business people, Canadians approach life more as employees—good employees, but employees nonetheless. The country is not devoid of small business activity; the small business sector is active, innovative and expansive. Rather, Canadian entrepreneurship, particularly of the small shop variety, appears to be quite restricted.

Canadians are, in contrast, quite enamored with franchises. A drive down any major urban street will reveal hundreds of franchise operations: hotels, restaurants, rental car companies, office supply stores, retail operations, corner groceries, video stores, clothing outlets and many others. Franchises dominate the shopping malls, and generally reflect US patterns. (Not all US franchises can be found in Canada, and there are a few franchises in Canada that are not yet available in the United States, but the pattern still holds.) The franchises offer a variety of attractive features: turn-key operations, market research, regional and national advertising, product selection, and commercial oversight. As a consequence, they carry less risk (and potentially lower growth potential) than self-owned operations.

Visitors will find many unique small businesses in the machinery, software, engineering, and manufacturing sector. Canadians are not without a capitalist spirit and there have been some major successes (including autoparts producer Magna, clothing manufacturing Peter Nygard, and the regional conglomerate assembled by B.C. entrepreneur Jim Pattison). There is, as well, considerable speculation in real estate (commercial and residential) and an entrepreneurial ethos in the mining sector. Many small companies have resulted from corporate restructuring and downsizing. Truckers who were once employed directly by logging companies are now self-employed entrepreneurs, and farmers are, of course, aggressive business people. Somewhat oddly, however, this only rarely carries over into the retail and service trade, where franchises dominated and are becoming more important over time.

The size of the Canadian market and the need to consolidate to produce economies of scale necessary to compete with US prices, push the country's business towards near-monopoly operations. Canadians are used to monopolies and oligopolies in many areas—energy and telephone services (until recently), department stores (where Eaton's, the Bay and Simpson Sears used to dominate), air travel, television, and many other sectors. At present, one company—Chapters—dominates the book industry, although it is challenged on a regional level by Indigo. Wal-Mart is emerging as the market leader in the low-end department store field. Air Canada dominates air travel, Tim Horton's and Starbucks lead in the cafe category. Only a handful of independents operate in the automobile service station area. Two cable companies—Shaw and Rogers—have divided up the country between them (and appear to be facing down competition from several satellite television providers). A few media companies have a hammerlock on the private distribution of news and entertainment.

Canada is a physically large country with a series of small, regional markets. Southern Ontario and, to a lesser extent, Vancouver, offer highly competitive environments with considerable opportunity for the development of new businesses. In much of the country, however, small-level entrepreneurship in the retail and consumer services areas is limited. It is, in consumer terms, a largely middle class country (parts of Vancouver, Toronto, Montreal and Calgary excepted) with rather basic tastes and demands. Canada is not a country noted for high-level products or a demand for the very best. Franchises, shopping malls and standardized products appears to serve the country quite well. Commercial battlegrounds tend to revolve around new franchises and chains seeking to enter an area rather than locally grown businesses rising up to challenge national or international companies.

Government and Business in Canada

Canada's political complexity creates considerable confusion for foreign business people. Some issues (patents, for example) are federal responsibilities. Others, such as minimum wage rates, rest with provincial authorities. There is, as a consequence, a complex regulatory, statutory and legal maze facing international businesses seeking to work in Canada. Given the fundamental importance of government in Canada—more so than in the United States, for example, it is important to spend a little time exploring the political structure of Canada and to examine the contemporary relationship between politics, government and business in the country.

Canadian Federalism

Canada is a federal state. The national government has a set list of responsibilities, which include criminal law, international trade and diplomacy, the maintenance of an army, the establishment of a central bank and currency, national parks, and the general regulation of the national economy. Provincial governments are responsible for attending to the more immediate needs of their citizens and manage education (including universities), social services, roads, municipalities, and health care. Over time, the federal government has also asserted a role in ensuring an equitable distribution of government resources and services in the country. As a result, it taxes wealthier provinces and transfers the money to the poorer jurisdictions. The national government has also asserted responsibility for maintaining uniform standards for such things as health care, human rights, environmental protection and the like. The system has shifted over time, with provinces occasionally transferring authority to the federal government and with the federal state surrendering some control to the provinces. In fact, the struggle to define the balance of powers between the national government and the provinces is one of the defining characteristics of the country's political life.

Within this system, the Prime Minister of Canada has extraordinarily strong powers. Members of Parliament—Prime Minister Trudeau once referred to backbenchers as "nobodies"—have very little authority and are expected to toe the party line (or face direct political consequences, such as removal from the party or the loss of the nomination in the next election). Elected officials exercise none of the freedom or independence that is typical in the United States and many other countries. The country's Senate is a largely irrelevant institution. Senators are occasionally rousted from somnolence on a specific issue, but the institution is typically ignored or sharply criticized by Canadians. The federal cabinet, made up of elected officials and Senators, sits at the pleasure of the Prime Minister. In practical terms, the Prime

Minister and his immediate office staff effectively set government policy in the country. Save for one or two key ministers, the Prime Minister generally operates with a free hand.

Opposition in Canada, such as it is, tends to come from provincial governments. While this is most notable in the case of Quebec, which has advanced the cause of separation with considerable electoral backing since the mid-1970s, other provinces generate their share of criticism and struggles with the national government. The battles tend to focus on national tax rates and payments to the provinces, particularly for health care, social services and education. The provinces meet on an annual basis and often unite to demand greater resources and autonomy from Ottawa. The federal government listens politely and then generally ignores the entreaties. There have been some great political battles over the years between the two levels of government: BC and the federal government over immigration, Alberta on oil and gas policy, Saskatchewan and Manitoba on agricultural subsidies, Ontario and Quebec on a wide range of topics, the Maritimes on transfer payments and regional economic development, and Newfoundland on fisheries policies. These battles were particularly prominent in the debates of the 1970s and 1980s over constitutional reform, and will remain a permanent feature of the Canadian political landscape.

In terms of business, the federal government plays a major role in shaping macro-economic policy: setting interest and tax rates, managing the currency (by allowing the dollar to float downward), establishing the rules around unemployment insurance, providing money for regional economic development initiatives, funding major infrastructure projects (which, over time, included the national railway system, the CBC, Trans Canada Highway, Saint Lawrence Seaway and, most recently, the country's excellent Internet backbone), and negotiating international trade agreements (such as NAFTA and the failed Multilateral Agreement on Investment). Provincial governments are more directly involved. They participate in the awarding of subsidies to business projects, establish provincial tax rates, control natural resource use, set local environmental, labor and other regulations, and work closely with small business development. Most businesses work far more intently with provincial governments than federal departments, but they operate within a fiscal, monetary and regulatory environment established by the national administration.

Provincial Competition
Because of the federal system in Canada, individual provinces exercise a great deal of freedom to develop economic strategies as they wish. Some, like British Columbia over the past ten years, put their faith in government-led growth; others, particularly Ontario and Alberta, emphasize the economic fundamentals (low tax rates, easy to navigate business regulations, strong infrastructure). What all the provinces do—sometimes with federal help—is compete against each other for business.

In past years— and some of this remains in place—there were strong barriers to interprovincial trade. Quebec, for example, strongly restricted access to provincial projects for construction companies and workers. The nation's brewery system mandated that beer had to be produced in the province in which it was sold, resulting in a network of small, inefficient and expensive breweries. For years, for example, Americans found it easier to purchase New Brunswick's Moosehead beer than did Canadians in western provinces. (This law was later eliminated, resulting in a rapid consolidation of the brewing industry and the closure of many provincial plants.) Interprovincial trade barriers attempted to protect local business, industry and services, but they contributed significantly to the cost of doing business in Canada. Efforts have been made to eliminate most, if not all of the trade barriers—to create, as it were, free trade within Canada—but parochialism remains a tough nut to crack.

In a similar vein, Canada's provinces compete aggressively

with one another for industry and major businesses. A foreign company seeking to do business in Canada will often find itself facing numerous suitors, each of them offering province-specific opportunities and incentives. Alberta promotes its low-tax environment, while Manitoba highlights its sustained, low hydro rates. The Maritime provinces have the opportunity to leverage federal money, and are quick with tax incentives and other subsidies. Quebec is determined to attract long-term business to the province and is prepared to work very aggressively to keep the province's industrial plant expanding. In 1999-2000, Quebec and New Brunswick squared off over subsidies and incentives to keep Lantic Sugar in operation. The company had two plants, one in each province, and had to close one. The provinces vied for corporate attention before New Brunswick finally called it quits, unable to match Quebec's generous offer. New Brunswick, in turn, earned the ire of other provinces with former premier Frank McKenna's aggressive campaign to attract firms—in this instance call centers—away from other provinces through a series of infrastructure supports and business incentives.

Visitors to Canada's booths at international trade shows will find ample evidence of this inter-provincial rivalry. Individual companies will, of course, bring their own displays and search for their own clients. But it is not uncommon to see the Canadian provinces opt for a competitive approach. Quebec usually goes it alone, as does Ontario. Alberta is expanding its international presence and often maintains a booth of its own. British Columbia used to do more, especially in Asia, but it appears to be cutting back its activity in recent years. The Maritimes are less likely to be present (and when they are, it is usually with federal assistance), but they tend to show up as a group. Canada is not unique in this. Australia often has state-focused displays and US states are known for following their own agendas in business development. For Canadian provinces, the inability to cooperate on international business development initiatives is quite consistent and results in the country presenting a fractured and unclear image to the world.

In the absence of a clear and consistent national business development strategy, something that the federal system in Canada does not permit and that provincial politics would not sustain, provincial governments vie with each to attract business. (This occurs within the province as well, as local economic development organizations compete with one another for industrial or commercial ventures that appear destined for their area.) Foreign companies have become quite adept at playing jurisdictions off against each other, and provinces have been known to go to quite remarkable lengths to attract additional investment. This competition works in the company's best interests. At least one international firm working in Quebec, not really needing any subsidies to justify an expansion of existing operations, nonetheless insisted that it be provided with the same kind of tax breaks and incentives provided to other companies willing to make major investments. To do otherwise, they realized, was to unnecessarily leave money on the table.

There is an imbalance in the subsidy and incentive wars. Alberta and Ontario are attracting a great deal of investment on their economic merits; both provinces will still participate heavily in negotiations with incoming businesses and will provide incentives and supports as required, but they are not as aggressive as in the past. Eastern Canada—Quebec, the Maritime provinces and Newfoundland—are the most subsidy-oriented, and the provincial governments have been extremely eager in their efforts to attract business. The effort has been an uneven success; many of the businesses attracted through the subsidy and incentive system have not thrived and closed their doors without producing lasting returns. For areas like rural Quebec, Cape Breton Island (which recently opened a large call center as a result of major federal subsidies), the Acadian peninsula and Newfoundland, the experience with recruited companies has been uneven. Manitoba, Saskatchewan and British Columbia are middle-rank players in the subsidy game, responding with business partners and investors to opportunities but not pursuing potential businesses with the same enthusiasm as the eastern part of the country.

Regional Economic Diversification
A major part of the business-government relationship in Canada is built around federal-provincial efforts at regional economic diversification. The economic realities in Canada are harsh and clear: three provinces prosper (Alberta, Ontario and British Columbia), three others are doing reasonably well (Manitoba, Quebec and Saskatchewan),and the other four and the three territories are lagging well behind. Canada has long had an economically activist state, committed to the idea of redistributing income between individuals and regions. For the past few decades, this has taken the form of substantial regional economic development programs, designed to create new commercial opportunities in the poorer parts of the country without, it is hoped, siphoning off business from the rest of the country. To critics, the regional economic development initiatives are pork-barrel politics at its worst, as large sums of money are allocated to regional ministers, who (opponents allege) are more interested in politically timely investments designed to win seats than in making appropriate investments. Supporters, on the other hand, argue that such initiatives are critical if disadvantaged regions of the country are to find the investment capital necessary to overcome historic and geographical barriers and become full partners in the nation's economic prosperity.

The regional economic development program currently runs in three arms: a program targeted at the ultra-politically sensitive market in Quebec, the Western Economic Diversification fund, and the Atlantic Canada Opportunities Agency. Each of these areas has a sizable annual budget, with an administrative unit and a federal political politician overseeing the effort. The program officials work with provincial authorities, local businesses, universities and other actors in the identification of opportunities and commercial prospects. The funds support infrastructure projects, training and promotion initiatives, grants to large businesses and small business loans and support. They are working, by definition, in difficult economic environments and are charged with creating economic growth in areas which suffer from a lack of entrepreneurial spirit or want of clear commercial openings.

Federal efforts at regional economic diversification cannot claim major success at the macro-level. Regional difficulties in Canada are quite entrenched—more on a sub-regional than a province or region-wide basis—and will take many years and much good fortune to set right. (Critics of these efforts claim that the government spends too much time trying to move work to the workers, rather than realizing that the economy generally requires workers to move to the work.) Great publicity follows the failures, of course, and when loan guarantees or subsidies are discovered to have underpinned a collapsed business enterprise, there is much criticism leveled at the program. In reality, each of the initiatives operates within a reasonably strict corporate frame of reference and produces a large number of small success stories.

Gaggle of Regulations
Most business people in Canada discover that the federal and provincial system adds considerably to the complexity of doing business in the country. The situation is not too difficult if operations are restricted to a single province. In such circumstances, the company finds that it has to cope with federal and provincial rules and, with the right professional advice, these can be easily navigated. Interprovincial operations present another set of challenges, however. The complexity of provincial regulations, legislative requirements and rules can add to the time and cost of doing business. Efforts have been made to streamline some of the regulatory systems and there are numerous professionals available to assist with the political and administrative

Harbourfront Center and Granville Island

Canadian critics often accuse governments of never getting their commercial investments right, and seem to assume that government involvement in a major project is almost certain to doom the initiative. There are, of course, contrary examples, two of the best being Toronto's Harbourfront Center and Vancouver's Granville Island Market. Harbourfront focuses on contemporary culture and provides a venue for music, dance, theater, readings, and countless other activities. It draws locals and visitors—more than three million per year—into the area and has played a pivotal role in rebuilding the commercial vitality of the Toronto waterfront. The centre has pride of place in Canadian cultural life and has proven the value of both cultural investments and government-private sector cooperation. Granville Island Market was a real shot in the dark in the 1970s. The federal government (which then managed Canadian harbors) proposed the development of a farmers' market on an industrial site in the middle of the city. The market was an early success with producers and consumers alike, and quickly attracted other activities. Warehouses were converted into work spaces for artists and craftspeople. Dozens of small stores opened up, as did restaurants, a theater, a hotel and a college of art and design. The surrounding land, largely neglected warehouse space, became prime residential real estate and soon became the site of numerous cooperatives and condominiums. Additional developments, particularly of the marina and retail facilities, followed. Granville Island Market, another example of government-cultural-private sector cooperation, is now one of the city's favorite attractions (although the original *raison d'etre*, the farmers' market, has taken a back seat to other developments).

environment, but the problem persists. For example, environmental regulations can differ quite dramatically from one province to another. So it is with wages, working conditions, medical plans and coverage, education and post-secondary systems, tax regimes and the like. There is, at present, no easy way around this matter in Canada and the federal system shows few signs of changing in the near future. In fact, if there is a political consensus on political structures in Canada it is more toward a loosening of the bonds of federalism and the granting of greater autonomy to provincial authorities.

The Great Canadian Tax Debate
Business people visiting Canada for the first time will discover that the country is engaged in a long and loud debate on the future of the Canadian tax regime. Superficially, Canadian federal and provincial tax rates are not competitive with the United States—something that the NAFTA and continental trade has made brutally clear to all business people. The reality is less clear, however, as Canadian taxes carry significant personal benefits, including excellent state-funded schools, colleges and universities, a good (but no longer excellent) health care system, and, until recently, little of the user fee structures that dominate US public services. The health care benefits alone are worth a great deal to the average family, although the actual benefit varies from province to province. In British Columbia, for example, there are annual premiums for health care. Saskatchewan has historically had higher tax rates than other western provinces, but there are no annual health care charges.

Nuances aside, Canadians are engaged in a vigorous public debate about the Canadian tax system. The Canadian Alliance Party, the official opposition but with few parliamentary seats outside of western Canada, advocates a flat tax system; the New Democratic Party, Canada's social democratic alternative, demands higher taxes on the wealthy (defined by the leader as people earning more than C$60,000 a year). The Liberal Party, in typical fashion, plays on both sides of the street. For much of the 1990s, the Liberal government accelerated taxes—and instituted a "wealth" tax on high income Canadians—and justified this on the need to pay down the annual deficit and to start reducing the nation's ballooning debt (over C$500 billion). In the 2000 election, facing rising support for the Canadian Alliance, the Liberals converted to a tax-cutting agenda, promising sharp cuts in personal income taxes in an attempt to become more competitive with the United States—and in recognition of the nation's success in fighting the deficit. (The tax cuts were less than the increases in tax rates over the previous decade, so personal and business celebrations were rather muted.) To confuse matters further, Prime Minister Chretien ended 2000 by musing about the need for a guaranteed annual income system and for sharp increases in spending to address poverty across the country.

Canada, then, continues to face the national conundrum: government spending to tackle the nation's social ills (poverty, regional inequality, aboriginal needs, women's issues and health care improvements) or tax cuts and a reduction in government services in order to make the country more competitive. The country is divided on a provincial level as well, with Ontario and Alberta leading the way on the tax cut agenda and other provinces favoring a more activist approach (and, to be true, lacking the revenues to support large tax cuts). Regional differences are beginning to be debated more openly. Western Canadians have begun to question the Maritimes reliance on federal transfers and their demands for more financial assistance. Eastern Canadians are nervous and angry about the western and central Canadian innuendo, which suggests that Atlantic Canadians are "lazy" and unwilling to work.

The thoughts of Canadian business are clear on this issue. Business organizations have steadfastly advocated greater and faster tax cuts, a reduction in the administrative burden, and less government in general. They have argued, in particular, that Canada continues to lose business and key personnel to the United States because of the federal and provincial approach to taxes and government regulations. They point, with justification, to less flexible arrangements in Canada on stock options, top tax rates and other provisions (capital gains taxes in Canada, for example, and mortgage tax deductibility in the United States) that make it far more attractive to work in the United States, particularly for high-income professionals.

The country's general trajectory is toward a more US-style tax regime, although it will take some time to get there. Canada's flirtation with high deficit, high debt politics made the entire nation nervous about continued government spending, and there was strong support for the idea of eliminating provincial and federal deficits (they are almost all gone now). The idea of paying down the debt is approached with less urgency, and Canadians appear to support the allocation of additional funding to the public sector, particularly health care. Continental and international trade, however, is making it increasingly important that Canada stay competitive in the tax field—and at present it lags behind the United States and most Asian countries. Pressure on governments to limit taxes and to reduce the role of government will continue, as is happening around the world in the age of globalization. Canadians will wrestle with this issue, for the country has long benefited, personally and regionally, from an activist state. Over time, however, it is likely that the low-tax, limited government model will win out.

Government Leadership on Economic/Business Matters

Business analysts have long debated the importance of government leadership on national business development. Through the 1980s and early 1990s, many analysts lauded the Japanese experience and came to believe that the capitalist development state model was the most successful in the world. Japan's recession in the 1990s and America's unrestrained commercial boom (until late 2000, that is) associated with the growth of the Internet challenged that model and resulted in sharp criticism of Japan and greater support for the more liberal, open-market approach of the United States. There is a US consensus on this issue—business is good, government is bad—but other countries do not yet share this enthusiasm for the unfettered marketplace. Moreover, the decline in the US stock markets and the end of the dot.com boom in the country might well lead to a quick questioning of the viability and transferability of the US model.

Canada has long taken a middle position on these issues. It has been open to international investment and foreign ownership. The country's richest citizens have only rarely provided much national leadership, and many of the most successful business people and companies have relocated to the United States or Britain. The federal government has played, as described above, an active role, particularly in regional economic diversification and transfers to individual Canadians. At the same time, however, the nation evidences little confidence in federal business leadership, and the sell-off of almost all of the country's leading crown corporations was not greeted by much in the way of protest. Canadians, it seems, want economic leadership but not federal interference; national support programs, but not state ownership.

Over the past five years, the federal government's approach has changed dramatically (and most provincial governments have gone along with the new direction). Led by Paul Martin, Minister of Finance and by far and away the most credible member of the federal Liberal government (exceeding, incidentally, the Prime Minister), the government shifted away from personal support and major regional development initiatives. Emphasis was placed, instead, on debt reduction and major federal investments in national infrastructure. The government made a substantial commitment to the Internet and information technology, provided millions of dollars for basic and applied university research, privatized major government facilities (including airports), and declared increased interest in international trade. The country has engaged, for the first time, in a lengthy dialogue about international competitiveness and there is growing understanding that the country has to operate on a global scale if it is to succeed economically. The enthusiasm for international involvement is tempered, as it should be, by concern about environmental protection and social justice, and Canadians will not soon surrender their interest in regional and personal equality. National interest, for example, in building a sustainable health care system remains very high and offsets the commitment to economic competitiveness.

Government matters in Canada, and businesses working in the country will spend a fair bit of time working with federal, provincial and municipal organizations. They still struggle with regulatory complexity and with the shifting division of activities between federal and provincial agencies. They may benefit from inter-provincial rivalries and will certainly need to explore regulatory differences in any provinces that they are considering for their operations. The system will cause frustration at times; it certainly has limited the country's ability to present a unified national business "face" and has often resulted in inefficient and unproductive competition between provinces and major cities.

At the same time, government is an important part of the Canadian business environment. The physical and social diversity of the country would never have been overcome without substantial government involvement in railways, telecommunications and social services. That there is a rough equality of opportunity in Canada is due in substantial measure to federal intervention and federal-provincial negotiations. Government support, subsidy and incentive programs underpin many successful foreign and domestically-owned businesses in Canada. And although business people often complain loudly about government interference in their affairs (they usually mean taxes, labor laws and environmental regulations), many will also tell you that provincial and federal officials work very hard to encourage local and regional business development. Far from being opponents of business, these government agents are often aggressive proponents of industrial and corporate growth. Canada has been blessed over the years with a highly professional, generally non-partisan public service; simplistic assumptions about government-business rivalries do not do justice to the degree of government-commercial cooperation and partnership that underlies business development in Canada

Canada does not offer one of the world's most competitive marketplaces. It is not the most innovative country or economy. It lacks the technical proficiency of Japan or Germany, is not as international in its outlook as Britain or Holland, and is not as dynamic as Hong Kong or as speculative as the United States. But—and this is a standard Canadian litany—it is a good country, with a strong economy, an excellent workforce and dependable consumers. Government and business cooperate, even if they do not innovate a great deal, and business people support the idea of a competitive, open commercial environment. There are few Canadian retail operations or, for that matter, products that have taken the world by storm. It is hard to get excited about international sales of coal, unprocessed lumber, pork bellies or wheat, even though these products are of critical national and global importance. The country receives more in the way of consumer products than it sells and tends to be a receptor nation in many aspects of its commercial life. As a place to do business, Canada is open, flexible, honest, and comparatively wealthy. It is a good test market for products aimed at mid-range, comfortable consumers—just as Japan and parts of the United States provide excellent places to test cutting edge electronics and high-priced goods. This may sound a little bland, but it is what Canadians are used to. It is also what Canada offers to the world: solidity, dependability, decency, and reliability. In the chaotic and ever-changing global marketplace, these are estimable qualities.

CHAPTER 4

Frozen Americans or Colonized Brits?: Cultural Aspects of Doing Business in Canada

Canada is a difficult country to figure out. The nation has obsessed for years about national identity and remains perplexed by its international diversity and lack of clear country-wide assumptions and values. This carries over strongly into the business world. Canadian business means working with Saskatchewan cooperatives and newly arrived Chinese entrepreneurs. It requires negotiations with branch plant offices and overseas owners. To succeed in Canada might involve lengthy discussions with competing provincial governments. The country defies easy characterization; it is not like Japan, China, or even Britain, where distinct and fairly constant commercial values and customs define the national business culture. It appears, from the outside, to be a more polite, less intense variation of the US model, for Canada shares a great deal in common with its wealthy, aggressive and domineering southern neighbour. This description of Canadian business culture must, therefore, be imprecise, for the absence of a set of core attributes is one of the key aspects of the national commercial system.

The Disappearance of the British Model
Until World War II, Canada was a strongly British nation. (French Canadians, living mostly in Quebec, did not figure prominently in national business. Anglo and Anglo-American owners managed most of the major industrial plants in Quebec and maintained considerable authority over the Francophone workforce. This

began to break down in the Quiet Revolution—Quebec's political turmoil—in the 1960s.) Imperial preferences and national choice tied Canada to the British market and the colonial "twinge" meant that gaining approval in the United Kingdom was the one true mark of individual success. Some Canadians did well. Lord Beaverbrook, for one, made a fortune in publishing in England and was widely honored in Canada for doing so. Growing ties to the United States and the emergence of the United States as a world superpower after the war weakened the ties with Britain and began to erode Canadian preoccupation with the British model. There was a time, however, when the business elite in Toronto and the English elite in Montreal made concerted efforts to replicate the habits of the British gentry and presented to the world a very British affectation.

Deviations from the US Model

Canada's growing ties with the United States after World War II created a conflict within the national business culture. American business people were very different from the often aloof and formal Brits. Fast-moving, loud-talking and aggressive, the stereotypic American business person bore little resemblance to his or her British counterparts. (It must be said, however, that the earlier American economic elite—the Rockerfellers, Carnegies, and the like—assumed the airs of the upper class rather nicely in their day.) US investments after World War II usually involved branch plants or direct management of Canadian plants, and the US partners typically monitored their holdings very closely. Canadians became, over time, more accustomed to dealing with the Americans. Proximity did not, however, generate imitation. In fact, Canadians have long defined themselves according to their differences from Americans and have clung to the thin threads of distinctiveness with uncommon determination.

International business people, however, often make the mistake of assuming that Canadians are really only slightly more polite variations on the US model. There are reasons why this would seem logical. There is a common language, and Canadians have access to US television, magazines, books and movies. A close inspection of Canadian and US groceries stores will reveal significant differences in product lines, but the distinctions are more those of brand name than substance. US restaurant chains can be found across Canada (although not all of them have prospered as Canadians are much less enamored with the fatty and greasy food that is standard fare with some chains). To make matters more confusing, it is not unusual to find an American business person working for a Canadian company, particularly in the senior administration. In recent years, Canadian investors seeking to protect their funds and Canadian companies wishing a more cutting edge, competitive approach to business have looked south of the border for leadership. In such situations, with an American in the top position, the line between Canadian and US business practices will blur even more.

Quebec Inc. and French Canadian Business Practices

Until the 1960s, the French Canadian business community was quite small. Prerogatives of languages and culture were used by the Anglo elite in Central Canada to limit French Canadian involvement in the senior ranks; Quebecois were expected to accept their working class lot, something that their Roman Catholic priests encouraged them to do. The Quiet Revolution in the 1960s changed the situation dramatically. Desperate to become *maitre chez nous* (masters in our own house), Quebecois threw off the shackles of a corrupt and domineering provincial government, elected a new Liberal administration, and launched a social revolution which targeted external control of the provincial economy, the educational and social power of the Catholic church, the domination of the federal government and, most importantly, Anglo control over the Quebec economy. What followed was a four decade-long struggle highlighted by the 1976 election (and repeated re-election) of the Parti Quebecois, a provincial party devoted to separating Quebec from Canada. After the first electoral victory, dozens of leading Canadian companies vacated Montreal for Toronto and other Canadian cities, sparking a prolonged recession and convincing many Francophones that their worries about Anglo-Canadian commitment to Quebec had been right all along.

While Canadians focused on the political unrest, a dramatic commercial revolution was taking place. The cornerstones of this revolution were three-fold: the activist provincial government which, after nationalizing Hydro Quebec, began to build a locally-controlled economy, the Caisse Populaire movement (credit union) which mobilized the savings of millions of French Canadians and made the money available for provincial development, and the emergence of a well-trained, outwardly looking entrepreneurial and business class. Initially derided for Francophone parochialism, the French Canadian business community merged into a powerful alliance of government and commerce, often referred to as Quebec Inc. This loose confederation of interests shared the goal of building a strong, locally-controlled, and international competitive business community. University students, for generations pushed by parents, church and the state towards the liberal arts, shifted into business studies, and upon graduation took a prominent role in the fast-changing Quebec economy. With Hydro-Quebec (and the huge James Bay project) fueling the expansion, Quebec Inc. developed a unique provincial business community, determined to take on the world.

The culture of the Quebec business community is, not surprisingly, different than the rest of the country. It is largely Francophone, although most business people are fluent in English as well. Quebec, like France, is very worried about the spreading authority of English and is determined to arrest its development. The province of Quebec has very strict language laws, which govern many aspects of business, including the posting of company signs, and these regulations are rigidly enforced. Language, obviously, is very important and is held up as the key to cultural survival.

The Quebec business leadership is mildly nationalistic. Quebec business people will not talk a great deal about politics and separation and will speak to the long-term stability of their community. The harsh edge that surrounded the separation issue in the 1970s and 1980s has dissipated significantly. They will point, with pride, to major, long-term deals with significant international businesses, each of which is presented as a sign of confidence in the province. But most Quebec business people are Quebecois first and Canadians second, and they will have made a strong personal commitment to the development of the provincial economy. If a political discussion ensues, you will probably discover that they are well-informed, good-humored about the issues, and far from doctrinaire or dogmatic about Quebec's prospects. They will also, like most French Canadians in Quebec, be distressingly confident about the inevitability of greater Quebec autonomy or independence.

The Canadian food retail sector is hotly contested and has generated great rivalries in recent years. Loblaws, with its headquarters in Toronto, operates a substantial grocery store network, including stores affiliated with Loblaws, Provigo (Quebec), Atlantic Save-Easy and The Real Canadian Superstore.

The Francophone business community is quite cosmopolitan in outlook. Dress, tastes in food, travel experiences and the like are more European than North American. Montreal and Quebec City are remarkably active and diverse cultural centers (Montreal has a very large Haitian population) and are worthy of considerable attention in their own right. The cities' cultural industries—theater, music, movies, publishing—are vibrant and very determined, for they are seen to be the vanguard of Quebec's struggle to assert itself culturally. Business people, in the main, are very French in orientation. You will find these business people to be more passionately local and regional than most Canadians, long-term in their thinking, and very competitive. They are internationalist in orientation, very competitive and innovative, and are driven to succeed. The success of certain sectors in recent years—aerospace, chemicals, engineering, transportation, and information technology—has added to regional confidence.

There is no reason to be wary about French Canadian business people, and the long-standing stereotype about Quebecois commercial backwardness (never fully true) simply does not apply. Quebec business people are professional, eager, and creative. They are anxious to position the province and the major cities at the cutting edge of the global and high-technology economy, and are determined to provide the economic leadership that the province requires. They are constrained, somewhat, by language laws and sensitivities surrounding Quebecois culture, but this is more than offset by the close cooperation between business, the Caisse Populaires (century-old Quebec-based financial cooperatives that have done much to mobilize provincial and Francophone investment capital), and the provincial government. Quebec is anxious to do business; for most international business people, the most significant adjustment one would have to make would be to get used to hearing English with a French accent and to experience some of the best restaurants in all of North America.

Canadian Business Culture

It is difficult to describe the Canadian business culture, both because it appears so close to the US model and because of its internal diversity. In fact, it is not clear if there is a national approach to business, but rather a commercial mosaic that reflects the country's ethnic, economic and geographic diversity. Italian-Canadian business people in Toronto work differently than fifth generation New Brunswickers. East Indian approaches to business in Vancouver bear scant resemblance to First Nations commercial styles. And the world-famous entrepreneurial habits of the Chinese outside of mainland China are well-represented in Canada, particularly in Vancouver and Toronto. In some ways, then, the concept of a "Canadian business culture" is something of an oxymoron. One of the most successful aspects of Canadian business is actually its multiculturalism and its openness to ethnic diversity. This generally applies across the board. Chinese traders are very familiar with Chinese practices, but they do not necessarily expect them to be followed in Canada. Greek businesses are run with full accommodation to Canadian standards. (One caveat; ethnically-based businesses working within their cultural community tend to follow business practices that are specific to that culture.)

Importance of Regional Variations

Along with the nuances of Canadian multiculturalism, regionalism is one of the most important national attributes. Regional business environments differ greatly. Vancouver is a unique business environment. It is at once the most Asian part of Canada and the most Californian. This is the land of lattes and hot tubs (often chided as being Lotus Land by other Canadians). It is edgy, youthful, and entrepreneurial—and many of its most important entrepreneurs are of Asian ancestry or are recent immigrants from Asia. As such, it has a complex commercial character that encompasses Asian business traditions, the wild speculative fervor of the Vancouver Stock Exchange, and the West Coast lifestyle embodied in the proliferation of Starbucks coffee shops and avant garde restaurants. Calgary, Alberta, in contrast, was once described as "Dallas North" and another time as "The most American city in North America." The oil and cattle city is hard-driving, entrepreneurial and fast-moving. US approaches are commonplace here, and it is a hearty, friendly and competitive city. Edmonton, only 2 1/2 hours' drive to the north, is the capital city, with the enthusiasm of the resource sector constrained by a stronger union movement and deeper social democratic roots. Both cities are "red meat" business environments, and are among the most competitive and entrepreneurial in Canada.

The other two prairie provinces, Saskatchewan and Manitoba, are less intense, more agrarian and calmer. Neither has shared in Alberta's resource boom or B.C.'s Asian immigration. Both have stronger social democratic political traditions (in 2000, both had NDP provincial governments) and very strong cooperative movements. As well, both provinces have very sizable Aboriginal populations and are struggling to incorporate these communities into the mainstream economy. Saskatoon is the most aggressive of the cities in these provinces, and has a flourishing bio-tech industry that holds great promise for the future. Regina, the provincial capital, is less connected to the global economy and moves at a slower pace. Winnipeg was a major Canadian city in the early twentieth century, and while it retains a cultural vibrancy, it has lost some of its commercial edge. Efforts to rebuild the urban and provincial economy have progressed slowly, although there are some substantial trading companies in the area.

Ontario offers, likewise, a variety of business cultures. Toronto's business environment is the most active in all of Canada (and Canadians are united, it seems, only in their "hatred" of Toronto and their envy of its success). Toronto is the hub of southern Ontario industry, is Canada's financial center, and has all the cockiness and brashness of the dominant city in the country. While it foolishly aspires to be a smaller New York, it can legitimately claim to be a world-class center, with remarkable cultural diversity that it has begun to exploit for commercial advantage. There is an arrogance and comfort-level in Toronto that irritates other Canadians; the city and its suburbs seems to assume that local prosperity equals national success and there is little evident concern for economic difficulties elsewhere in the country. Hamilton and Windsor are heavy industry, company towns, with strong union influences; efforts to expand their commercial reach have not been all that successful. Ottawa, in contrast, has remade itself. This long-sleepy capital city was reinvented by the information revolution. It is Canada's version of Silicon Valley, home to major high technology firms (Nortel and Corel, for example) and a hotbed of new economy start-ups.

Leaping over Quebec (see the discussion above), one comes to the unusual and bewildering commercial environment of Atlantic Canada. This once bustling region wallows in continued hard times. Part of the challenge rests with historic divisions; the area has a population of less than three million, but maintains four provincial governments. The Atlantic region has become the butt of Canadian jokes, most implying laziness and unwillingness to work, and has become the target for increased criticism in recent years. Halifax, the largest city, is a vibrant port with a strong academic and administrative environment. The business culture here is comparatively laid back, somewhat government dependent, and not yet nationally and globally competitive. Saint John, New Brunswick, is the most active industrial city in the region and works very hard at commercial development. It is saddled with perennially bad political representation and seems incapable of catching up with the times. Moncton and Fredericton, in contrast, are both more aggressive and coordinated and, in the current environment, more successful than Saint John. They have done well in attracting new economy investments. Charlottetown, Prince Edward Island, is a pleasant provincial capital but it lacks the vibrancy (and airline connections) to attract much outside interest. St. John's, is the center of the perennially struggling Newfoundland economy. While the city has benefited from the expansion of the oil and gas industry, the area remains burdened with the legacy of a dependency culture. Government officials, however, work hard with local entrepreneurs to create opportunities, but opportunities have proven to be few and far between.

Economic dependency runs ever more deeply across the Canadian North. The territories function only with massive transfers from the federal government. Recent declines in the resource sectors have harmed regional business greatly and spurred a flight of capital, commerce and personnel from the territories. Aboriginal land claims settlements have spurred First Nations and Inuit businesses, but local conditions have again conspired to limit their profitability. The North, even more than Newfoundland and the Maritimes, is a subsidized economy, and commercial and government leaders work with the assumption in mind that government financial support is essential for business development to occur. This means that external businesses often secure financial backing, but also places government officials in critical roles in determining the pace and nature of commercial activity. Logistical and geographic barriers severely restrict regional business opportunities, and the local commercial culture reflects the bitter experiences of an economy shaped by short-term booms and long-term busts.

There is, obviously, no single Canadian business culture. Each region of the country, and each major city within the region, carries the burdens of history and economic realities and the opportunities presented by local cultural diversity. There has been considerable movement across the country—many Newfoundlanders have moved to Alberta to find work, and New Brunswickers routinely leave the province upon graduation—but the regional business environments have remained quite resilient. Your approach to business, obviously, must be influenced by the focus of your attentions. It is important to learn more about the nuances of

Arctic Cooperatives

Inuit carvings and prints are among the most famous of all Canadian art works, and enjoy strong international markets. This is a fascinating industry, created with government assistance in the 1950s and 1960s, and flourishing through to the present. Behind the sculptures and printmakers rests a most critical enterprise—the Arctic Cooperatives Limited. While cooperatives assist in the creation and distribution of Inuit art, the over forty members of the Arctic Cooperatives Ltd provide even more basic services. They form, in fact, the background of the retail and consumer service sector in much of northern Canada. Member organizations—organized on a community by community basis but working cooperatively on a regional, national and international level—operate most of the local retail stores, hotels, gasoline and heating fuel distribution, local and regional shipping, housing rentals, travel services, cable television, and the like. The cooperatives are also extremely active in community development, leadership and management training, and local business promotion (working closely with the NWT Cooperative Business Development Fund). Most of the political leaders in the Northwest Territories and Nunavut spent at least some time working with cooperatives, which are both deeply ingrained in village and reflective of the community spirit which influences Arctic society.

regional business cultures, for the value systems, assumptions, attitudes and approaches to investment, trade and entrepreneurship vary widely from coast to coast to coast in Canada.

Branch Plant Mentality

Since the late nineteenth century, Canadians have welcomed US and other investors to build branch plants within Canada. Initially, this investment came so that producers could gain access to the Canadian market, protected by high tariff barriers from imports. More recently, the branch plants have been built by companies from Japan and Europe, using NAFTA regulations to enter the US market while capitalizing on lower Canadian costs. In either case, this has meant that many of the largest companies in Canada have long been foreign owned, and were managed either by imported business people or by locally-hired managers. This pattern created a branch plant mentality, whereby Canadian managers were constantly looking outside the country for leadership, advice, or approval. It created, in the process, a reluctance to take leadership positions and assert control of the local operation. Branch plants ship profits, expertise and knowledge back to the home office and to the main manufacturing operations; in the process, they can also stifle initiative, require Canadian nationals to work under other cultural business regimes (i.e. US or Japanese), and develop an ethos of commercial and managerial dependency on the head office managers or the owners.

Risk Aversion

While there are many very successful entrepreneurs in Canada, the country is actually quite risk averse. Canadian business tends to move cautiously, reflecting the experiences of the past and an ingrained lack of confidence in the likelihood of commercial success. As a nation, Canadians prefer the tried and the true to the adventurous, and it is often difficult to convince corporate leaders and government officials to head off in a new and risky direction. This approach to business rests on the country's long-standing reliance on the resource trade: a relatively straightforward, simple and easily understood commercial sector. Markets either opened or closed, prices rose or fell. The nuances of consumer preference, changing tastes, or innovative new technologies did not really apply to wheat sales, the lumber trade or efforts to market Canadian iron ore and coal. There is a tendency, as well, to mock speculators and risk-takers and to take no small measure of satisfaction from their fall from grace. (British Columbians followed, with some glee, the rapid change in fortunes experienced by real estate investor Nelson Skalnbania, as did Albertans when Peter Pocklington's long run of commercial success ran out, as Ontarians did when Michael

Cowper's dramatic achievements with Corel ran into hard times.) Canadians tend to be more bureaucratic, safer and risk averse in their investments and approach to business. One hopes that the aggressiveness of recent Chinese and other immigrants will rub off on the domestic business community over time.

Limited Risk Capital
Canadian business has trouble finding risk capital. Through a combination of national mindset (see the discussion on risk aversion above) and Canadian tax regulations, Canadians do not make a great deal of risk capital available to entrepreneurs. The nation's banks, although very profitable and with large pools of investment funds, are loathe to move rapidly into new areas, and most of the country's major entrepreneurs take a limited role in encouraging other commercial development. Not surprisingly, the contrast between Canadian and US approaches to investment leads many Canadian entrepreneurs to move quickly down to the United States in order to exploit the more fluid capital markets and to capitalize on the highly (sometimes wildly) speculative commercial environment south of the border. Of course, once they do so, these entrepreneurs tend to keep their operations in the United States, meaning that Canada loses out on the economic and employment benefits from such investments.

US-envy
Canadian business people have a very complex attitude toward the United States. Many of them do a great deal of business south of the border, and most of them admire the United States' commercial accomplishments. More than a few each year relocate to the United States and capitalize on lower tax rates and generally higher rates of pay; many thousands spend most of their annual holidays in the United States. Canadian business people, as well, hold the United States in some awe; the country's truly impressive economic performance in recent years has stood in sharp contrast

to Canada's less dramatic growth rates (which Canadians know is largely due to US expansion) and lesser level of prosperity. They pressure the federal government to match the United States' tax regime and commercial environment, and threaten to relocate (themselves or their company) unless Canadian conditions improve. Envy runs deep in the Canadian business community, and almost all of it is pointed at the risk taking, entrepreneurial, and innovative business world in the United States.

At the same time, however, Canadians love to point out the United States' shortcomings. Canadians took great delight in President Bill Clinton's infidelities and in the political charade that followed the Lewinski revelations. Along with the rest of the world, they mocked the United States for the failings of its electoral system in the 2000 presidential elections. They have long chided the country for its militarism and history of racism, fretted about right-wing fanaticism and US hypocrisy in global politics, and openly criticized the country's love of firearms. Canadians love to laud the benefits of Canadian medical care and the limitations of the United States' vastly expensive for-profit system, and complain about the US lack of compassion for the poor and the homeless and the mindlessness of US popular culture. They are, implicitly, celebrating the fact that Canada is more equitable, more just, more sophisticated, more compassionate, better governed, and less racist than the United States.

(One shortcoming that brings particular delight, rather oddly, is the fact that Americans pay virtually no attention to Canada and know very little about the country. A popular national television program routinely mocks the United States by sending a camera-crew to interview people on the sidewalks of major US cities. The people are either asked a series of very basic questions about Canada—which virtually none of them can answer—or are presented with a ludicrous statement about Canada and asked to respond (For example, would they sign a petition to stop polar bear hunting on the streets of Toronto.). Canadians, in some perverse twist of national character, find it outrageously funny to discover that their partner in the world's most important trading relationship knows virtually nothing about them.)

The most significant element of the Canadian interest in the United States, however, has to do with the Canadian inferiority complex. Since Confederation, Canadians routinely compare themselves to the United States and, just as routinely, find their country wanting. The United States has always been richer, more powerful, more attractive, more innovative, more competitive, more risk-taking — in general, more of just about everything. To Canada—an impressive nation by global standards—this reality has long meant that Canadians see their business community as a faint shadow of the US miracle, almost a failure by definition. Canadians, therefore, are ambivalent toward the United States, laud its commercial accomplishments, mock its political life, and highlight its social limitations. But, more than anything, they will evidence a clear desire to emulate the economic success and the business environment of the United States.

Limited Internationalism

Outside the immigrant communities (a large and growing sector), Canadian business is decidedly not very international. Most of the country's trade is with the United States, and it is soon easy to see why. Ready access to the large, dynamic and open US market has made Canadian business quite complacent. A concerted effort is made to crack into US business, but this extends very little to other countries. Most Canadian business people have limited international experience, rarely speak a language other than English, and show little interest in the complexities of international trade. They do not, as a group, pay a great deal of attention to world affairs and show little signs of expanding the nation's commercial horizons. This is starting to change a little, particularly in select sectors such as engineering, high technology and architecture, where Canadian firms are making a significant international name for themselves. But across the board, Canadian business tends not to have the global outlook of, say, European, Japanese or Hong Kong business people, or even the understanding of broader forces that one might find fairly commonly in Australian companies.

Heavy Reliance on Government and Foreign Investors

The combination of a risk averse nature, limited risk capital and uneven economic development has encouraged Canadian business people to rely heavily on others. A plethora of government business subsidy programs has encouraged a generation of Canadian business people to look quickly—sometimes too quickly—for federal or provincial subsidies, to rely heavily on officials for advice and assistance, and to count on external money to underpin commercial ventures. Oftentimes, very good projects go awry because of the complexities of bureaucratic and political interference; conversely, some very poor projects can be rushed to the front of the commercial queue in order to meet a political or regional agenda that has little to do with good business. At the same time, the willingness to share risk with outsiders, many of whom have a broader, international perspective on the business opportunity at hand, means that Canadian businesses end up surrendering a sizable portion of the profits and control to non-Canadian investors. The risk aversion that is so evident in Canada can result in a cautious approach to business that limits the effectiveness of sound entrepreneurial instincts.

"Nice" Business People

International business people routinely comment on how "nice' Canadians are and how easy it is to deal with them—less rigid than the Japanese, less competitive than Indians or Pakistanis, more reserved than the boisterous Americans, and less driven than the hard-dealing Chinese. It is a pleasant (and accurate) description of the country's business people, although it lacks a certain edginess and suggests that Canadian commerce is perhaps a tad less assertive and direct than that found in other countries. What it means, positively, is that Canadian business people tend to be not terribly aggressive, reserved in their commercial dealings, and extremely friendly with newcomers and international colleagues. While the country offers up its share of sharp talkers, back slappers and cheery well-wishers, most Canadian business people are relaxed, quiet, and very open.

Trust

Canadian business people tend, as a group, to be very trustworthy. There are, in this country as elsewhere, exceptions to the rule. The international controversy over the BREX mining company, a Canadian firm found to have soared in value on the basis of fraudulent samples from an Indonesian mine, is very much the exception in Canada. The country's commerce is much less litigious than in the United States (largely due to a legal system that discourages the commercial contests that are commonplace in the United States), although it appears to become a little more so with the passage of time. The country does not work on the basis of a handshake and a promise; lawyers are an integral part of the commercial process in Canada. But the country and the nation's business people are widely known for the level-headedness of their representatives, the high level of responsibility to clients and partners, and strong respect for contracts and the law. The avoidance of wild speculation, in this instance, has the added benefit of creating a business environment founded more on solid evidence than false promise.

Informality

Business relations in Canada do not have the sense of ceremony and formality that is normal in Asia, nor the rigidity that is commonplace in Europe. The country falls, in fact, midway between Europe and the bonhomie of the United States. Canadian business people tend to be sensitive to matters of culture (as it relates to their trading partners), but unlikely to stand on ceremony for themselves. Most people within a company work on a first name basis and most commercial transactions operate in a similar manner. There are no explicit rules, as in Japan, for how to conduct meetings, greet visitors, shake hands, present cards, or otherwise handle business affairs. Canadian business meetings tend to be very relaxed, and most executives are easy-going and informal. Some quick suggestions: be punctual, do not assume Canada is part of the United States, and do not be too indirect nor too direct in your business dealings with Canadians.

Socializing and Gift-Giving

Canadian informality carries over to after business activities. It is not uncommon for Canadian business people to show off their city or region to visitors; they are proud of the country's physical beauty and have learned that visitors often enjoy seeing the countryside. Excursions to viewpoints, lodges, golf courses, or other such "escapes" are quite routinely worked into business activities, again particularly when foreigners are involved. There are no formal requirements about exchanging gifts as part of commercial dealings, but presents are welcomed and will often be reciprocated. (Canadian business people are getting better at learning the habits and activities of their trading partners and are becoming better prepared at welcoming foreign visitors.) After work drinks are very common, although drinking to excess is very rarely part of the agenda. Canada is becoming increasingly health conscious and there are both strong laws and intense social disapproval associated with drunk driving. Most business people will avoid the risk of such a problem. Furthermore, family considerations are becoming increasingly important in Canada, and business people are more likely now than in the past to be alert to the need to get home to see their spouse and/or children. Do not be surprised if business people cut short their business day in order to spend time with their families.

Women in Canadian Business

Thirty years ago, women legitimately complained about wage and employment discrimination in Canada. While the problems are not entirely gone—women still face the problem of glass ceilings (ie. running up against barriers that they cannot see)—they have moved aggressively and successfully into the Canadian business world. The business world is not equally divided between men and women. Most senior executives will be men, mostly in their 50s and 60s. But international business people should expect to encounter many women in their dealings with Canadian business—and they will be found in all aspects of the company's operations. A few Canadian males still complain about affirmative action programs and corporate hiring policies deemed to favor women, but these assertions are becoming increasingly anachronistic. Women, with very few exceptions, are in place on merit. They make up a significant majority of the country's university students, are showing up with increasingly regularity in the graduating classes in such non-traditional areas as engineering, accounting and law, and have demonstrated, across the nation, a remarkable level of interest in self-employment and small business development. Most Canadian companies have developed policies designed to suit the professional and personal needs of women, including good maternity leave provisions, corporate day care programs, and greater flexibility in defining jobs and work requirements. While still some way behind some of the Scandinavian countries in terms of the country's ability to incorporate women into the workforce, Canada has responded quite creatively to women's demands for commercial opportunities. Perhaps most significant in the long-term, women are becoming increasingly active as entrepreneurs and are thus showing up with increasing regularity on the ownership side of business.

Ethnic Minorities in Canadian Business

The situation facing ethnic minorities in Canadian business runs roughly parallel to the experience of women. Long-term patterns of discrimination have been the focus for aggressive government policies and concerted minority protest. Over time, some ethnic groups (Japanese Canadians, Chinese Canadians, Canadians of Eastern European ancestry) have been able to find or create excellent opportunities for themselves. Barriers still exist. Recent immigrants, including those from the Caribbean, South America and Africa, complain of resistance in the workplace. Some companies, particularly in the Toronto area and British Columbia have learned the value of including people of various linguistic and cultural backgrounds in their workforce and have created strongly multicultural corporations. Do not be at all surprised to find Canada's cultural mosaic represented among the employees and senior executives of your Canadian partners.

Aboriginal Business in Canada

One group, the aboriginal people of Canada, are not yet well-represented in the workforce or the business community. Most indigenous settlements have extremely high rates of unemployment and poverty is endemic across the First Nations reserves. The federal government has attempted to encourage aboriginal economic development, with a sad lack of success over the years. This said, a small group of aboriginal business people has emerged, capitalizing on the resource wealth of their communities and/or drawing on the resources available through land claims settlements. In a few areas, most notably British Columbia, the Canadian North, and Alberta, resource-rich reserves are creating their own businesses, employing First Nations people, and seeking to establish international markets for their products and services. The whole area of aboriginal business is grossly underdeveloped—the most successful indigenous operations in many parts of the country are government-sanctioned gambling casinos—and government is continuing to offer financial assistance to aboriginal people who are attempting to launch a business. Most international business people working in Canada will encounter few if any aboriginal businesses. Companies working in the resource sectors, in contrast, will find that they will have to devote an enormous amount of time, energy and money to meeting with and understanding aboriginal aspirations, needs and conditions. In western and northern Canada, aboriginal communities have negotiated successful joint venture projects and have become directly involved in resource development; they are not, as some observers fear, automatic opponents of commercial activity in their traditional territories. Aboriginal commercial aspirations and operations promise to figure more prominently in the future, and companies seeking to work in Canada, particularly in northern and remote regions, had best be prepared to spend considerable effort on their relationships with local and regional indigenous groups.

Canadian business defies easy characterization. It is the antithesis, in some ways, of the rule-laden Japanese or Chinese business environment and more complex than the open, free-wheeling US commercial world. Complexity—shown in cultural and regional diversity—is the cornerstone of the Canadian system. Moreover, the Canadian business environment is uniquely Canadian. It is no longer a faded version of the old British system, and has not been for several generations. Nor is it a failed variant of the United States, although the deeply entrenched habit of self-criticism has convinced many Canadians that their country falls far short of the US model.

Canadian business culture is, in the end, a fascinating blend of regional variation, ethnic difference, historical patterns, and

Indigenous Resource Rights

Aboriginal rights issues are becoming increasingly important in Canada and business people are paying closer attention with each passing year. In British Columbia, province-wide land claim negotiations have stalled a series of major development projects, as companies wait for a resolution of modern treaty talks. In September 1999, the Supreme Court of Canada ruled that the Mi'kmaq of the Maritimes had an existing treaty right to fish for commercial purposes. The treaty right rested on agreements signed in the 1760s. The Marshall decision, as the ruling is known, created shockwaves in the region and resulted in widespread protests. Local non-native fishers feared for their livelihood and the federal government struggled to keep a lid on potential difficulties. While short-term resolutions were secured for most of the First Nations groups, the long-term impact is uncertain. The Marshall decision may, for example, apply to other resources, including forestry. Aboriginal people will certainly become more prominent in the regional fishing industry—they made substantial strides in the lobster fishery in 1999–2000—and this in turn may start to address their long-term isolation from the commercial economy in the Maritimes. Non-aboriginal fishers believe that Mi'kmaq gains will come at their expense and that their communities will suffer economically in the years to come. The Marshall decision is but the most recent example of the clarification of aboriginal resource rights and the resulting attempts by First Nations and governments to negotiate a peaceful, fair and sustainable distribution of harvestable, commercially-valuable resources in Canada.

modern social relationships. Canadians are, as a group, a profoundly nice people, known for a genuine friendliness that is masked somewhat by national caution and reserve. It is a business culture that recognizes and acknowledges diversity, both internal and external, and that is surprisingly open to newcomers. And it is also a business culture that lacks confidence, that lives too much in the past and shies away too much from the future. It is a business environment that demands that government get out of the way of their operations, and that nonetheless turns to government too quickly for support and protection. Canadian business operates in the shadow of the world's largest economy and, in a commercial burst of national envy, routinely declares itself to be a second tier nation, unmindful of the fact that such an attitude becomes a self-fulfilling prophecy.

CHAPTER 5

The World's Most Important Trading Relationship: Canada-US Business

If you ask Americans, including leading government officials, to identify their most important trading relationship, they will invariably say "Japan." And they will be wrong. The most important commercial partnership—in the whole world—is that between Canada and the United States. Canadian export to the US total more than 80% of the country's total. US firms are, by far, the largest investors in Canadian companies and own large sections of crucial Canadian industrial and resource sectors. Even before the advent of the Canada-US Free Trade Agreement, the two countries' economies were significantly interwoven.

Canadians are constantly offended by the United States' lack of understanding of Canada's commercial importance to their country—and even more distressed by the limited US awareness of Canada's existence. To Americans, Canada is responsible for the Arctic fronts which deliver intense cold and snow storms to their country and for most of the hockey players in the National Hockey League. Even well-educated Americans only laugh when confronted with their profound ignorance of Canada. The reverse is not true. Canadians travel to the United States regularly, follow developments in sports, popular culture and current affairs. Most Canadians know as much about US history as their own, and follow US politics with as much, if not more, enthusiasm that Americans do. Canadians might hold overly cynical views of the United States, but the level of national understanding, particularly among the university educated cohort, is quite dramatic. No major trading relationship in the world is based on

Few young Canadians remember that Tim Horton was a famous hockey player with the Toronto Maple Leafs. What all Canadians do know is that Tim Hortons is a coffee and donut chain which is particularly popular in Eastern and Central Canada. Tim Hortons merged with Wendy's, an American hamburger restaurant chain based in the United States, in 1995. The company operates over 2,000 stores, all but 115 of them in Canada.

such an imbalance in understanding and concern as is the Canada-US partnership.

The disregard rests, in part, on the implicit assumption that Canada is simply an extension of the United States. In the 1980s, an US presidential candidate was asked about his country's energy security. He observed that the United States had lots of oil, in Alaska, California, Alberta and Texas—and there was only a slight snicker among observers when it was pointed out that Alberta was a Canadian province, and not a US state. George W. Bush provided two further examples of this profound ignorance during the 2000 election campaign. A Canadian comedian, posing as a journalist, informed Bush that Prime Minister Poutine had endorsed his candidacy. (The Prime Minister of Canada was Jean Chrétien; poutine is a French Canadian food, consisting of gravy and cheese curds on fries.) Bush expressed his appreciation for the support, as did his advisors when questioned subsequently. Even more importantly, the would-be president made a point of phoning President-elect Fox of Mexico to congratulate him on his electoral victory. No such call was made to Prime Minister Chrétien when he won re-election in November 2000.

Regardless of the cultural politics of the situation, daily trade between the United States and Canada fuels the economies of both nations. Thousands of trailer trucks and railcars move north and south each day. Hundreds of business travelers cross the border on commercial missions. Cross-border ownership and stockholding buttresses companies in both countries. Canadian resources, particularly timber, pulp and paper, natural gas, and electricity, underpin US industry. And since the nineteenth century, huge migrations of people from Canada to the United States and from the United States to Canada have intertwined the countries in ways that have enriched both. US tourists vacation in the thousands across Canada, and hundreds of thousands of Canadians travel south each winter for a respite from northern cold spells. While Americans appear to have little difficulty understanding their economic and social development without reference to Canada, it is not possible to come to terms with Canadian business without exploring the nature of the Canadian-US commercial relationship.

History of Economic Ties
In some ways, Canada exists as a repudiation of US values. The Loyalists and French Canadians who shaped Canada's development in the 19th century did so with clear attention to the failings of the US experiment. It proved to be a difficult task. Many thousands of those who migrated to British North America in the early 1800s stayed but a short time before pressing on to the more promising opportunities in the United States. But there was a reverse migration as well. Settlers from New York pushed across the Great

Lakes and inhabited the rich farm lands of what is now Southern Ontario. But British North American looked to Britain, and sought economic solace in British protectionism, relying on the government to hold US competition at bay. There was considerable cross-border trade and contact, but British North America was determined to develop separately from the United States.

From the middle of the nineteenth century, Canadians have debated the merits of greater commercial ties with the United States. For many years, the protectionists held power, and used the authority of the British government and, after 1867 the federal government, to build protectionist barriers against US commercial incursions. The result was not as expected. US firms crossed the border and built branch plants to service the Canadian market, providing jobs and spending money but selling goods to Canadian consumers at higher prices than those available to the south. A sharp political division emerged. The Conservative Party led by John A. Macdonald wrapped itself in the British flag and pledged to maintain Imperial preferences and economic separation from the United States. The Liberal Party was more continentalist, and urged greater integration with the United States. Whenever the issue surfaced, which it did with some regularity, the question of economic relations with the United States touched off heated national debates across Canada. The matter arose, most dramatically, in the 1911 election, with Prime Minister Wilfrid Laurier pledged to knock down protectionist walls and build a cross-border economy. Conservative leader Robert Borden promised to hold the course, and to remain loyal to Britain. In a bitter and divisive election, the Conservatives swept into office, thus stalling the integration option for the time being.

Because economic relations between the two countries strengthened over time, it stood to reason that the issue would arise again. William Lyon Mackenzie King, perhaps the most continentalist of Canadian Prime Ministers, tried to push the cause, but with little success. After World War II, general prosperity and growing Canadian industrialization masked the question of Canada's long-term relationship with the United States. But tensions during the 1960s over the war in Vietnam and US anger about Canada's criticisms sparked an increase in economic nationalism. Canadians worried about increased US investment in Canada and the potential loss of control over national resources. The Liberal governments of Prime Ministers Pearson and Trudeau made some minor moves toward greater national control, including increased review of foreign investments in Canada. But these did more to slow down economic growth than to increase Canadian economic independence. To the more cynical, the issue had become moot. The United States' power was so immense and Canada's so minimal, that there was little the country could do save to leap into bed with the United States.

Eyes Wide South

Looking to the United States for Economic Salvation: The 1980s were difficult years in Canada. Federal government spending in the 1970s, designed to build national prosperity, had done nothing of the sort. What it had done was build a huge national debt—among the highest in the industrialized world—and a staggering annual deficit. The country emerged from a period of sky-high interest rates into an era of stagflation: high unemployment, continuing high interest rates, and very slow economic growth. Government spending was clearly not the answer, but the alternative was not altogether clear. Prime Minister Mulroney, first elected in 1984, struggled unsuccessfully with government spending and turned the government's eyes instead on the negotiation of a free trade deal with the United States. Mulroney, like King before him, was familiar with the US scene and comfortable working with US business people. He encouraged economic integration and clearly envied the United States' continued economic expansion. Canadian economic inferiority, always a key aspect of the nation's approach to business, peaked in this era, as the country appeared to be bedeviled by political woes and long-term economic burdens. Access to the US market was offered as a salvation.

Canada-US Free Trade Agreement/NAFTA

The negotiation of a free trade deal became the focus of Canadian government efforts in the 1980s. In contrast, it scarcely registered on the political and economic radar in the United States. The situation again irritated Canadians. On one side of the border, the population debated a matter of intense national importance; the 1988 election was, at once, the most principled and the most emotional in years, for Canadians were genuinely divided about the issue. Proponents spoke of untold prosperity, as Canadian firms sold goods and services into the US market and as US firms brought cheap goods north of the border, driving down consumer prices in the process. Opponents were less optimistic. Labor unions declared that wages and benefits would fall to US levels, undercutting the middle class prosperity of Canadian workers. Supporters of Canada's social programs declared that a free trade deal would force Canadian governments to end income supports and the nation's valued health care system. Environmentalists worried about legally mandated water exports, a siphoning of Canadian resources into US markets and a lowering of national environmental standards. Shrill and angry protesters—led by Liberal leader John Turner—asserted that a free trade deal would effectively obliterate the Canada-US border and result in the elimination of Canadian distinctiveness.

No political accord could ever deliver such amazingly positive benefits or ruinous consequences, and certainly not at the same time. Negotiations plodded along under the cloud of Canadian debate and the fog of US ignorance. (A few Americans were concerned, mostly those with strongly protectionist leanings who feared the loss of US jobs and business in an openly competitive market. Despite external appearances to the contrary, the United

States hosts a solid undercurrent of suspicion about open international trade, and there is a solid constituency in the country that surrounds the "US first, last and always" ideal.) It was not as if the countries were starting from scratch. The Auto-Pact agreement struck in the 1960s had permitted a version of free trade in auto parts between the countries, underpinning a large, successful automobile industry in southern Ontario and southern Quebec. By 1988, a tentative agreement had been reached—an immense and complicated document that contained, most critically, an opting out clause that either country could institute upon six months' notice.

The Mulroney government won the 1988 election and the Canada-US Free Trade Agreement was passed. The sky did not fall overnight, as some had predicted, nor did economic nirvana miraculously appear. The free trade agreement improved cross-border access and made it easier (but not completely easy) for Canadian firms to do business in the United States. Professionals found it easier to migrate across the border—largely North to South—and consulting, engineering, legal and architectural firms discovered important benefits in the accords. Canada attracted more investment, particularly from Japan, from companies anxious to gain access to the US market while retaining the benefits of the Canadian social safety net and government support system. Canadian firms discovered new opportunities south of the border, but also found the United States to be an intense and competitive market, with a very different ethos than Canada. Canadian Tire, a national hardware and auto supply store, made an extremely expensive foray into the United States, only to retreat before the venture swallowed the entire firm. US firms had long been active in Canada, and the agreement made their work somewhat easier. But the benefits were small and long-term rather than dramatic and immediate.

From the beginning, the United States had been interested in extending the free trade agreement south to Mexico. Canada concurred and negotiations commenced on what would eventually become the North American Free Trade Agreement (1994). The old debates were joined again, with Americans taking far more interest in NAFTA than they had in the original accord. Industries worried about the rush of factories to the cheap labor and regulation-free environment in Mexico. Canadian and US producers wondered if they could compete with products produced in such a setting. Human rights activists and environmentalists claimed that the negotiations represented an end-run around human dignity and environmental protection and would result in the exploitation of Mexican workers and the further despoliation of Mexico's physical setting. Northern trade unions protested vigorously, and in vain, against the idea, believing that they would lose thousands of jobs. (Their points were countered by business people who claimed that global competition was eliminating the high-paying, low skilled industrial jobs, and that those companies were fleeing to Asian countries already.) The politicians prevailed, and NAFTA was implemented.

NAFTA, like the Canada-US Free Trade Agreement before it, turned out to be a significant contributor to economic development, but was neither the panacea or the disaster debaters had suggested. By the early 1990s, prosperity returned to the United States with a vengeance. Driven by the expansion of the digital revolution and the emergence of the Internet as a formidable economic force, the US economy expanded in leaps and bounds. Protectionist forces in the countries, which had organized in angry protests over the initial NAFTA deal, were silenced by the onset of good times. Even more, the anticipated mass migration of jobs to Mexico did happen. Some companies, Canadian and US, moved south and prospered in the low-wage environment. Others, including a few which relocated, discovered that salary costs were but a small part of the productivity equation, and either reopened their Canadian or US plants or maintained their existing workforce. The introduction of computerization and other efficiencies ensured that all three countries did better in the years after the free trade agreement was implemented.

US Interest in Canadian Business Opportunities

While it remains true that Americans pay precious little attention to Canada, the same is not true of US business people. The Canadian market has long been attractive to US companies: it is, after all, close, accessible, easy to enter and culturally similar. Moreover, the availability of a well-trained, reliable and hard-working labor force has long convinced many firms to establish operations in Canada, where their employees benefit from the (less costly, to employers) benefits of the national welfare system. (There are sensitivities behind US assumptions about Canada. A few years ago, a US bookdealer was visiting Canada and commented to a local publisher, "This is a fine market you have here." The Canadian responded, more than a little bitterly, "We prefer to think of it as a country.") The opportunities in Canada, particularly after NAFTA, include the following:

1. Canada provides an excellent base for manufacturers wishing to serve the US market. The provisions of NAFTA and a long history of close relations and cross-border trade has made it very easy for US companies to consider Canada as a location for manufacturing operations.;
2. The country offers a market of 30 million largely middle-class consumers, with tastes quite similar to those in the United States;
3. Cross-border sharing of television programs and continental circulation of magazines (and, to a much lesser extent, newspapers) means that advertising aimed at the US market filters into Canada.
4. Canada's large and accessible resources provide excellent opportunities for US firms seeking to ensure a steady and reliable supply of raw materials for their factories and plants.

US newspapers, for example, often maintain long-term deals or ownership positions with Canadian pulp and paper mills in order to secure continued access to newsprint.

5. The decline in the value of the Canadian dollar has meant that Canadian wage and benefit rates are falling relative to the United States, giving the country a cost advantage in certain manufacturing areas. The availability of national health and other benefits also means that US firms do not have to—as they do in the United States—provide private health care coverage.

6. Canada's wilderness areas are particularly attractive to Americans, who live in a more crowded and developed country. US purchases of Canadian rural and cottage real estate are extensive; Prince Edward Island has gone so far as to impose restrictions on non-resident land ownership in order to slow the rate of US purchases.

7. Despite a few political uncertainties, especially surrounding Quebec, Canada is one of the world's most peaceable and stable countries, thus providing a safe location for investment and manufacturing activity.

8. Americans face few difficulties entering Canada, and cross-border investments are readily facilitated by a large group of Canadian lawyers and accountants specializing in Canada-US relations. (There are two matters that travelers should pay very close attention to when crossing the Canada-US border. Canada has very rigid regulations governing the possessions of handguns and unlicensed rifles and enforces them very thoroughly. Similarly, the United States has a no-tolerance approach to the importation of illegal drugs and is very unforgiving of people who break the rules.)

9. Cross-border personal relationships are very strong. The historic pattern of migration between the two countries, with large numbers of Americans entering the prairies in the early twentieth century and coming to Canada in the 1960s and early

1970s, and with a steady flow of Canadians to the United States over the years, means that personal, family and professional relationships across the border are among the strongest in the world. This is particularly true in the Maritimes, Ontario and Alberta, and much less so in Quebec and British Columbia.

US interest, in Canada, therefore, makes a great deal of sense and remains a prominent feature of the continental economy.

Direct US Investment in Canada

Americans control very significant portions of the Canadian economy. From time to time, the level of direct US investment in Canada has generated a nationalist backlash, but even soaring levels of US ownership in recent years has failed to produce the normal reaction. Canadian companies are, thanks to the low value of the dollar and the comparatively weak national economy, inexpensive to outsiders, and Americans have stepped in to expand their holdings of Canadian firms, particularly in the resource sector. Many long-time national stalwarts, like British Columbia's Macmillan Bloedel (a forest products company now owned by Weyerhaeuser), have Americans as majority stake-holders. The country's Foreign Investment Review Board was significantly weakened following the advent of the Canada-US Free Trade Agreement and NAFTA, and there are few official or public protests surrounding continued US purchases of Canadian companies.

There is an inescapable logic behind the pattern of US investment. US investors have vastly more capital than Canadians, and are more willing to tackle risky opportunities. Combine this with the US desire to secure access to resources and the stability of the Canadian market, and it makes sense that US funds would flow over the border. Many of the investments are in major manufacturing plants, particularly in the southern Ontario automobile sector, where billions of dollars in new construction have sustained the region's economic booms. Financial deregulation, which is proceeding somewhat slowly in Canada, has attracted some US interest. Other major investments are in such old stalwarts as mining and forestry. New economy sectors, like information technology and digital infrastructure, have likewise attracted a great deal of interest.

Direct US investment will continue and, if the dollar continues to weaken and the US economy remains strong, will likely expand. The integration of the two national economies has proceeded apace through the twentieth century and, despite occasional Canadian protests, is almost certainly to continue. At times, some Canadians become either frustrated with their country's limp response to foreign/US ownership and raise their voices in protest or get excited about the prospects for closer ties and propose even more dramatic political measures to draw the economies together. US commentators sometimes dismissively refer to the country as the "51st State," a statement which irritates Canadians no end. To be dominated economically by another country is one thing; to be virtually ignored by the United States in the process only adds to national frustration and unease.

Canadian Investment in the United States

If government regulations permitted, Canadians would invest far more money in the United States. Millions of Canadians maintain registered retirement savings plans, which afford a means of deferring income tax on current income and providing for post-retirement expenses. Under existing regulations, the federal government permits individual account holders to invest no more than 25% of their total portfolio outside of Canada. This provision has done much to provide investment capital for Canadian companies, and has been behind the rapid growth in the Canadian securities and investment industry (and, more directly, behind the financial strength of such companies as Nortel. Before the stock price fell dramatically late in 2000, this single company was responsible for over 30% of the value of the Toronto Stock

Exchange and much of the increase in the TSE index over the previous two years.). But there is no doubt that, without these regulations, Canadian investors would greatly favor US stocks over local companies.

As it is, Canadians invest heavily in the United States. Individual investment accounts, not subject to the RRSP restrictions, are often weighted heavily toward US firms, and Canadians shared in the euphoria and, in late 2000, horror of the dot-com revolution. (It needs to be said, however, that Canadians are more risk averse than US investors and their response to the speculative nature of IPOs and dot.com stocks in general has been more cautious than in the United States.) Hundreds of Canadians, including people of relatively moderate wealth, own property in the United States. Many resort areas—Maui (Hawaii), Palm Springs, Phoenix, Arizona and environs, and significant sections of Florida (which is especially popular with French Canadians)— attract thousands of Canadian time-share owners and property owners. Wealthy Canadians often maintain residences in the United States and spend a great deal of time in the country. This is particularly true of the many Canadians who have prospered in recent years in movies, television and professional sports; they quite routinely point with pride to their Canadian roots but maintain a year-round residence in the United States.

Canadian investment proceeds on a broader scale as well. The country provides billions of dollars in direct investment capital. Canadian companies have been involved in major manufacturing operations (the core of Nortel's operations are now in the United States), urban developments (including large projects in Los Angeles and New York), real estate, mining, and other sectors. Canadian retailers have attempted—with very little success—to enter the US market. A few have succeeded, but efforts by Canadian Tire, Shopper's Drug Mart, and Future Shop, three of the country's most successful chains, foundered.

The shriveled Canadian dollar—which, it is important to note, is not an issue which has attracted as much national debate as one might expect or created widespread anxiety—has encouraged those with investment funds to move much of their money south of the border. As well, all Canadian banks now provide the option of maintaining accounts in US funds, a simple palliative that allows individual Canadians to operate as currency speculators. Discussion has increased in recent years about either creating a North American equivalent of the Euro or, even easier, adopting the US dollar as Canadian currency. While the predictable nationalist response has dampened the debate somewhat, the issue will not soon go away. Mobile professionals, led by entertainers, athletes and finance personnel, typically demand payment in US funds (this has recently been extended to the salaries of faculty members at a few Canadian business schools). The currency issue will not soon go away, and the likelihood of more and more Canadians holding their investments and savings in US funds as a hedge against the further decline in the Canadian dollar will probably spur additional debate.

For most Canadians, North America is now a single investment and retail market, with Canada's differences more akin to those of a region than a country. Developments in the United States have an immediate impact on the Canadian economy and stock market, and economic ties between the countries make it easy to do business across the border. Moreover, the comparative strength of the US economy and stock market has only added to the attractiveness of US investments. Canadian professionals know the United States intimately; it is unlikely that any other country has as many leading business and professional people with such extensive understanding of another nation; not surprisingly, many attempt to turn this insight and contact into personal and corporate advantage.

The Canadian Brain Drain

For the past five years, Canada has been locked in a bitter debate about the nature and extent of the loss of talent to the United States. Newspapers and television programs routinely report on yet another prominent or promising young Canadian "lost" to the United States. The list is extensive: top graduates from Canadian law and business schools, newly graduated engineers and computer scientists, leading Canadian academics and university administrators, prominent business executives, doctors, nurses, performers, and wealthy investors. There are stories, too, of companies like e-Bay and Home Grocer, that could not find risk capital in Canada and relocated to the United States where they found the money and established their operations. There is the reality that several major US centers—Silicon Valley, Los Angeles, San Antonio, Texas, Boston, Massachusetts—have attracted large numbers of Canadians.

Canadians have long been attracted to the United States and the greater wealth and perceived opportunities in the country have drawn Canadians southward for generations. Some twenty years ago, the United States government announced that they were going to hold a lottery for the highly desired Green Cards, which allowed immigrants to work in the United States. In Vancouver, applicants were invited to come to the US consulate to pick up an application form. On the appointed day, a huge crowd—estimated to be close to 5,000 people by some observers—milled around the consulate and rushed the door when the office opened. Appalled by the surge—something officials expected in developing world countries but not in Canada—consular representatives threw hundreds of applications into the air, leaving crowd members to fight for the highly valued "lottery" tickets. The scene was hugely embarrassing to many Canadians (some of whom pointed out that many of the applicants were newly arrived immigrants who had come to Canada only as a second choice to their preferred destination) for it highlighted the seemingly insatiable national

Canadians in the City of Angels

Canadians have long been lured by the economic and social magnetism of the United States. Since the nineteenth century, large numbers of Canadians have migrated southward, attracted by the stronger economy, greater personal opportunities and better climate. The pace of migration has increased in recent years, with many thousands attracted to the vibrant, dynamic and warm Los Angeles area. The exact size of the expatriate Canadian population in the region is not known, and the number fluctuates significantly with changing economic conditions in the Los Angeles area and in Canada. The attraction of the area continues to grow. The most high-profile migrants work in the music, television and movie industry—all areas where Canadians have done quite well in recent years—but many others have come for jobs in industry, finance and the retail sector.

The migrants have not cut ties with Canada—in fact, they are often fiercely loyal to their homeland. There are a series of organizations, including Canadians Abroad (Los Angeles area), Hollywood Maple Leaf Group, and Canadian Society of Southern California, designed to offer social and cultural activities for expatriates. As well, inexpensive air travel between Canada and the United States makes return visits easy. Moreover, the migration appears to be increasing rather than slowing, thus ensuring the steady expansion of the Canadian population in the region. Within Canada, the Great Vancouver and Toronto areas attract a large number of mobile professionals, but even these impressive Canadian cities cannot compete with the lure of Southern California and Los Angeles, despite the often bad press this city receives. There is, it seems, no Canadian substitute for palm trees, snow-free winters and year-round sunshine.

infatuation with the United States. For a country that celebrated its high standard of living and quality of life, and that touted its moral superiority to the United States (over such issues as health care, race relations, approaches to poverty and violence, etc.), the crush of would-be migrants was a severe scar on the nation's self-confidence.

Over the last ten years, aided by the easier immigration provisions facilitated by NAFTA, the migration has accelerated. The new economy, in particular, has attracted thousands of skilled personnel to the opportunities in the United States. The United States' advantages in this area are quite clear—more risk capital, more favorable tax and employment regulations (especially concerning tax rates on stock options), higher incomes, stronger currency, greater upward mobility, better government fiscal situation, and the many benefits of being in the world's most dynamic capitalist economy—and little has been done to arrest the movement. Small improvements in Canadian tax rates in 2000 helped a small bit, but did little to address the growing opportunity gap. Less mercenary, the United States offered Canadians in such key sectors as information technology, e-commerce, animation, bio-technology, health research and other areas unparalleled opportunities. World class research labs at the leading US universities vastly outstripped what Canadian universities could offer most of its faculty. Major US corporations, particularly in such fields as pharmacy and bio-technology, offered research money and facilities that Canadian scientists could only dream about. At the corporate level, the fast-moving, risk-taking environment, fueled by seemingly inexhaustible amounts of investment money, proved extremely attractive to Canadians frustrated by the more conservative and risk averse national business system.

The situation is not all one sided. The Canadian government has rushed to point out the northward migration of Americans, particularly into business and academic positions, and the fact that Canada has benefitted from an enormous "brain gain" from immigrant producing countries like India, South Africa, Hong Kong, China and eastern Europe and Russia. The losses to the United States, they claim further, are not necessarily permanent (the implicit assumption being that Canadians will return to the kinder, gentler country after a few years' experience of the harsher edge of the United States, an idea with a substantial element of truth in it, particularly as Canadians living in the United States realize the costs of health care for seniors). With immigration running at over 250,000 people per year and with federal regulations placing greater and greater emphasis on the technical and commercial skills of applicants, the government was confident that immigration would compensate for the loss of tens of thousands of Canadian scientists, researchers, specialists and entrepreneurs to the United States.

The truth remains elusive. At one level, there is no huge shortage of skilled workers in Canada (save in the same highly specialized areas that challenge all countries struggling to remain competitive in the new economy). Canadian universities produce enormous numbers of graduates each year—fewer in the sciences than the country would like, but well-trained nonetheless—and many of them struggle to find decent employment upon graduation. If there is a major shortage of workers in Canada, it tends to be in skilled industrial trades. Companies can find workers, even if they have to invest a fair amount of time and money in retraining them for corporate purposes. People lost to the United States are fairly easily replaced and often by people of comparable quality. Moreover, there are a large number of very talented, highly mobile professionals who are not attracted by the entreaties of the United States and who wish to remain in the country.

Still, critics of current government policy assert, the question is one of quality, not quantity (although critics do not surrender the statistical arguments so quickly). Anecdotally, some of those lost to the United States are the very best and brightest, in business and industry now as it has long been in entertainment and professional sports. US firms recruit at the very top end of the graduation class and seek the very best and most innovative technicians and executives. The country's loss, then, is not simply a matter of numbers but of lost entrepreneurship, diminished creativity and inventiveness, and reduced risk-taking, with those looking to live life on the professional edge heading to the United States. In this area, the argument is more compelling, for senior executives and top-flight personnel do significantly better in the United States and are finding options to the south to be increasingly irresistible.

There is a more insidious and significant process underway. The most successful Canadian companies maintain operations in both Canada and the United States. In an age of email, cell phones and inexpensive air travel, place of work and residence is becoming less and less important. Presented with the option of staying in Canada or moving to the United States—as an increasing number of Canadian executives have been—a growing percentage are opting to move. Canadian stereotypes about the United States being more violent, less equitable and with lower quality health care and schools do not hold when benefits package include first-class private health care, access to excellent public or private schools, and the social comforts of US suburban life. In these situations, executives are not being asked to choose between Canadian and US companies (their employer could be either), but rather strictly on the basis of preferred residence. When, as appears to be happening, increasing numbers are opting for the United States on the basis of lifestyle, earning potential and quality of services, Canada should be worried.

The Canadian brain drain is, at one level, the inevitable result of living close to the world's strongest economy and most enticing country. Nations the world over worry about losing key personnel to US firms, albeit at much lower rates and across a much narrower band of specialities. The United States is a powerful magnet, the attraction as much illusory as realistic. Popular culture weighs heavily in such circumstances, and entrenched images of US prosperity, opportunity and lifestyle seem unusually attractive when compared to the staid, slow-moving, government-dominated situation in Canada. Even though Canadian conditions have been changing, the shift has not kept up with the increase in US opportunities. Canada faces a serious problem in this regard, and the situation is driving demands to lower tax rates, reduce government interference in the economy and to liberalize even further an already open business environment. The country will do so only reluctantly; old and new images of US inequality, racial tensions, urban poverty and the like make the US model quite unattractive to a nation that prides itself on providing greater equality of opportunity and circumstances.

The Canada-US economic relationship is arguably the strongest, most peaceful, most reliable, and most comprehensive in the world. It angers Canadians that Americans assume that their ties with Japan are larger and more extensive and frustrates the country that Mexico generally attracts more attention than their country. Canadians know a great deal about the United States; US lack of understanding of Canada is profound and startling. The inequality of the relationship—the United States is far more important to Canada than Canada is to the United States — has limited Canada's options dramatically. Equally important, major improvements in the United States over recent years—New York is no longer locked, in Canadian eyes, in a permanent crime wave, and the United States is doing a better job of providing for the poor and disadvantaged—have chipped away at the veneer of Canadians' self-righteousness. In the past, the country could explain away its weaker economic performance by pointing to its greater decency, equality, and concern for social services and health care. Major reductions in Canadian services have reduced the differences dramatically and have undercut Canada's right to be sanctimonious on this account. (Fortunately, for Canadians, there is still the US preoccupation with firearms.)

Most Canadians, however, wish to emulate the United States' economic success and envy the level of personal opportunity and standard of living south of the border. Over the past decade, Canada's relative standard of living has fallen significantly, thanks in large measure to the government's willingness to permit the dollar to fall to historic lows, and America's prosperity has increased. While the United States does not always share the benefits of economic growth very equitably, the reality is that middle and upper class Americans are significantly better off than their Canadian counterparts and the gap continues to grow. Among Canadian opinion leaders, the desire to copy the United States' path to success is very strong, resulting in pressure for lower taxes, greater financial freedom and a reduced role for government. Many have voted with their money by shifting investments to the United States; others have taken the more dramatic step of relocating to the United States. Both processes, combined with increased US ownership of significant portions of the Canadian economy, are sure to result in continued integration of the continental marketplace in the coming years and to closer economic and social relationships between the world's two closest nations.

CHAPTER 6

Future Business Opportunities in Canada

Foreign business people looking at Canada from afar tend to see simple things: snow, ice, cold weather, trees, fields of grain, minerals, water, beef and fish. Canadian business is defined internationally by the country's physical characteristics and its resources. But Canada is also home to a high technology sector that, in select areas, is among the best in the world. It has a formidable and talented industrial labor force, an impressive (by European and North American standards) work ethic, and an ethnically diverse and globally connected population. Canada is strategically located next to the United States, with ready access to the world's largest economy, and between the European Union and the mega-markets of Japan and East Asia. It offers, as well, clear air, cheap land, abundant water, a solid if quirky political system, a high level of stability (aboriginal protests and the threat of Quebec separation notwithstanding), great respect for the rule of law, internal peace, and one of the world's most positive international reputations. When the list is compiled, it is difficult to identify a country with as many advantages, fewer substantial liabilities and greater commercial prospects.

But something is clearly still missing, Outside of select areas (southern Ontario, Montreal, Alberta and Vancouver), the nation's economy limps along instead of sprinting forward. Large sections—Newfoundland, the Maritimes, rural Quebec and rural Ontario, much of Saskatchewan and Manitoba, and non-metropolitan British Columbia—enjoy little or no economic growth and struggle to hold their own. It is not for lack of trying.

Canada's cities are modern, cosmopolitan and attractive environments—far removed from the stereotype of a land locked in winter and holding to a frontier past. Modern skyscrapers dominate the skyline in downtown Vancouver, the third largest city in Canada.

Federal and provincial economic development programs attempt to build regional infrastructure and create jobs, local development initiatives attempt to lure industries into depressed areas, and Canadian companies seek to secure financing to tackle new economy and old economy opportunities.

Saint John, New Brunswick, for example, has worked extremely hard to offset the closure of the city's shipyard and severe downsizing in the industrial sector. Efforts to attract new business have been, at one level, amazingly successful, building an entire new industry around call centers and information technology. At the end of the day, however, this decade-long effort managed to do little more than replace the lost jobs with positions that paid significantly less. A much touted effort to build a free trade zone and to attract foreign investors to a location with ready access to the US and Canadian markets, close proximity to North America's largest refinery, and a ready supply of natural gas still sits on the drawing boards, three years after it started. Close cooperation of local and provincial governments and the active involvement of Saint John business and, in many cases, organized labor, has not yet resulted in major investments or a re-orientation of the urban economy. A similar story can be told about Cape Breton Island, St. John's Newfoundland, Sherbrooke, Quebec, Brandon, Manitoba, Prince George, British Columbia and many other towns and cities across the country.

There are enormous commercial opportunities in Canada, many of them little known outside Canadian and select international circles. Canada is, it seems, a victim of its historical reputation and contemporary tourism marketing campaigns. The country aggressively promotes wilderness experiences and the wondrous beauty of the Canadian outdoors. In the process, they undercut efforts to market Canada as an emerging high technology power and do little to support the notion that the country is economically engaged in the world economy. Images of Mounties on horseback, mountains, moose, polar bears, ice-covered Arctic

Islands, and vast forested expanses do wonders for tourism and also promote the image of a country that is not connected to global developments. The "real" Canada, of course, is a more complex and diverse place, filled with commercial opportunities and business challenges, and very open to international investors and business partners.

Hollywood North: Entertainment Industry

Canadians have always been big movie fans, but never more than at present. One of the additional attractions in recent years has been that new Canadian game, "Watch my home town on the movie screen." The combination of a declining Canadian dollar—which has made Canadian facilities, staff and equipment decidedly cheaper than in the United States—and the development of technical proficiency in the movie sector have contributed to the rapid expansion of the Canadian movie industry. Much of the work is concentrated in Vancouver and Toronto, although major television and movie productions have been undertaken in all other parts of the country. The transformation has been dramatic, with numerous series (including the world-famous *X-Files*) being filmed on location in Canada. Canadian cities now routinely host major movie stars, and cope with the interesting frustrations of having portions of the city roped off for camera work. The result has been the development of a large, highly skilled and greatly appreciated technical corps in Canada. These technicians (and, to a lesser extent, actors as well) are greatly appreciated by the largely US firms that have relocated their filming operations north of the border. (Hollywood unions, incidentally, have taken note of the significant shift to the north and have protested the flight of work to the "cheap money" environment in Canada. Producers point out that filming in Canada can save 20% or more on a multi-million dollar budget—and Canadian film crew and other technicians provide first-rate service.) Canadian film companies and technical staff have attracted some non-US work, particularly in the making of television commercials, and there is optimism that the combination of technical proficiency, excellent locations for filming, cooperative local governments, and provincial and federal government subsidies will continue to keep Canadian film-makers active and profitable.

The Business of Culture

Culture is an important business in Canada, and the country hosts a full array of theater troupes, symphony and chamber orchestras, dance groups and other such performers. Government overwrites the costs of concert halls and theaters, and private sector firms provide substantial sponsorship to the groups and to major festivals. The biggest ventures—folk festivals in Vancouver and Edmonton, Montreal's full slate of summer festivals (comedy, jazz, film and others)— attract thousands of tourists and represent a major infusion of income into the local economy. One of the most successful ventures is the Stratford Festival, founded in 1952 and held annually in southern Ontario. The festival runs a full slate of Shakespearean productions, Canadian drama, and other musical and theatrical classics. It draws thousands of paying customers from southern Ontario and the northern United States and is one of the province's most important tourist attractions. While the primary motivation behind the Stratford Festival is artistic— and the performances attract world-class actors and directors—the success of the venture over the years has convinced other parts of the country to provide government and corporate support to cultural ventures.

Canada's contribution to the entertainment sector is not restricted to the movie industry. Before the 1970s, Canada's music industry was moribund. There were a few Canadian musicians who attracted international attention (Anne Murray, Paul Anka and the Guess Who), but the sector was small and far from the necessary critical mass. The introduction of Canadian content regulations in the 1970s, which forced Canadian radio stations to play no less than a fixed amount of Canadian music, force-fed the industry. Over the next twenty years, Canadian music developed into a first-rate cultural export sector. In the late 1990s, several of the top-selling artistes in the entire world (Celine Dion, Bryan Adams, Shania Twain and Allanis Morrisette) came from Canada, and Canadian acts were routinely breaking into Asia, European and US markets. In the process, these artistes developed a strong, technically proficient recording industry and provided a firm foundation for future generations of performers.

Global Circus

One of Canada's leading cultural exports—after popular musicians like Celine Dion and Shania Twain—is the remarkable cultural enterprise, Cirque du Soileil. Combining the showmanship of the circus with the frenetic nature of street entertainers, Cirque was launched in the mid–1980s. The organizers combined acrobats, dramatic music, wild costumes and fanciful story lines into a most improbable commercial success story. By the end of the century, Cirque du Soileil maintained seven shows, three permanent shows and four touring, and routinely playing to sell-out houses. In a dramatic shift that has the potential to transform Cirque into a global brand name, the company announced in 2000 that it was planning to open huge entertainment complexes. The goal is not to emulate existing entertainment centers—like Disney World—but rather to fuse their avant-garde performances, with retail operations, dining and other recreational activities. The first complex was announced for an abandoned power station in London, with complexes soon to be developed in other major centers. Cirque du Soileil retains its Montreal base of operations, but has developed a global reach, drawing performers from around the world and marketing its presentations from Asia to Europe.

Diamonds in the Tundra: Resource Opportunities

Diamonds, the world over, are associated with De Beers and with South Africa (and, to insiders, with other African countries and

Russia). There was considerable surprise, therefore, when news surfaced of the discovery of major diamond deposits in Canada's Northwest Territories. The Ekati mine (other properties are under development), opened only after careful assessment of potential environmental damage and negotiations with First Nations in the area. The companies have opted to market the gemstones (industrial diamonds are marketed differently) on their own, and not as a part of the De Beers cartel; the companies believe, rightly so it appears, that there is a distinct market for diamonds that are not associated with the racial and political unrest of Africa and that, instead, have the imprimatur of northern Canada.

The discovery of the diamond mines is an important reminder to potential investors. Canada remains a resource-rich country. Much of its vast Arctic and sub-Arctic expanse has not yet been fully explored. There are major deposits—including a huge iron ore deposit in the northern Yukon—that have been identified but not yet developed. Contemporary international pressures—the opening of mineral activity in South America (particularly Chile), Russia and elsewhere—has temporarily rendered some Canadian properties unprofitable. Furthermore, international concerns about Canada's high environmental standards and the potential disruptions relating to aboriginal land claims has scared some investors away. Several years ago, the government of British Columbia closed down two major resource projects—the Kemano Completion Project and a mine in the Tatshenshini River areas— largely due to environmental issues and in the face of some First Nations opposition. Business concerns, clearly, are not completely unfounded. Over the long haul, however, the value of Canadian resources will likely increase. The diamond mines provide a crucial indication of the potential importance of continuing exploratory activity and of the possibility of working with First Nations and regional governments to overcome social and environmental questions.

Canadian Power: Energy Industries

Canada has enormous energy reserves. It has large quantities of natural gas and oil off the east coast, in Alberta and Saskatchewan, and in the Canadian North. The country's hydroelectric potential is staggering. Major dams are in operation across the nation, with large quantities exported into the United States. There is, as well, the huge Athabasca tar sands, a vast expanse of oil-bearing sand in Northern Alberta that, alone, could support Canada's energy needs for many years (albeit at very high prices). Canada has, as well, a large (but not vibrant) nuclear energy industry, based on the CANDU reactor. Not all the country is equally blessed. Newfoundland's Hibernia field is just coming on line, and the Sable Island project off Nova Scotia is only now beginning to deliver natural gas into the region (ironically at a time when soaring gas prices are convincing many consumers to shy away from the service). Energy costs in Nova Scotia, PEI and New Brunswick have historically been very high, and Ontario and Quebec rely heavily on gas imported from western Canada.

The energy field, however, remains a Canadian strength. Oil and gas exploration continues in western Canada and on the east coast (but not as aggressively in the North as a few years ago). Canadian petrochemical companies, particularly in Alberta and Ontario, seek to add value to oil and gas products. Companies in Quebec, Manitoba and British Columbia have capitalized on the availability of comparatively cheap energy. A few companies, like Alcan, even own their own generating capacity and, when they have surpluses, sell the energy into the provincial electrical grid. Spin-off and service companies abound, and there are many opportunities in the exploration, development and application of Canadian energy resources.

High Technology

Canada is not well-known for its high technology sector, even though Canadians love to boast about the accomplishments of its major companies. The country is surprisingly active in high technology, and across such diverse fields as animation (for movies and games), communications infrastructure, consumer applications, and next generation products. Canadian firms are among the world's best at deep sea submersibles, Internet switching gear, and home-based telecommunications. Two companies, Nortel and JDS Uniphase, have been at the cutting edge of the Internet revolution. Nortel, generally seen as a US company, and JDS are among the world's most important Internet infrastructure firms, with contracts around the world and with major manufacturing plants in Canada and internationally. Vancouver-based Ballard, in contrast, is working on next-generation automobile fuel cells (hydrogen based) and is generally regarded to be the single most important company working in the area. At the point at which its products become commercially viable—and Ballard is working on prototypes with many leading car manufacturers—the company will become globally recognized for its contributions.

There are a few concentrations of high technology expertise and production—Ottawa/Kanata, Kitchener-Waterloo, Calgary and Vancouver—with areas like Fredericton, New Brunswick making a determined effort to join them in the big leagues. Canada's strong network of universities, federal and provincial commitment to high technology and the information revolution, and a small but growing number of Canadian firms devoted to developing national expertise auger well for the future of this sector. There is, of course, the countervailing threat of the United States, and the fact that risk capital is much easier to find south of the border. The country has already lost numerous entrepreneurs and hundreds of technicians to the greener pastures on Silicon Valley, California, Seattle, Washington, Boston, Massachusetts, and San Antonio, Texas. Continued bleeding for expertise, entrepreneurship and creative business ideas might well sap the vitality from this critical sector.

Service Sector

Canadians know very little about the international reputation and reach of its service sector. The country's strong and stable banking system, largely protected from international competition by federal regulation, has a truly global reach (although the federal government's refusal to accept the mergers of several of the largest banks will certainly undercut the presence of Canadian financial institutions in the aggressive international marketplace). While Canadian finance does not compete with London, New York or Toronto for the world's attention, it is nonetheless an active global player. In other service areas, notably engineering, and architecture, Canadian firms are the front-rank on the world scene. They compete successfully for major projects in Europe, the Middle East and Asia, and have undertaken some of the most important urban construction projects in New York and Los Angeles in recent years. Montreal-based Lavelin, for example, has extensive operations outside the country and is highly regarded for its engineering expertise. Canadian professionals have discovered that Canada is an excellent base for truly international operations, and have capitalized on the country's reputation for integrity, reliability and cultural understanding to sell their companies' services in countries across the world.

Agriculture and Bio-technology

Canadian agriculture is no longer the engine of national development and has (see below) fallen on hard times. At the same time, however, Canadian research on agriculture has placed the country at the forefront of bio-technology research, particularly as it applies to food products. (Canadian research on human aspects of bio-technology is quite strong as well, with major centers of activity in Toronto and Vancouver.) Clusters developing around the University of Saskatchewan and, to a lesser extent, the University of Guelph in Ontario are pushing Canadian frontiers in this important area. For over a century, Canadian scientists have contributed to the sustainability and commercial viability of Canadian agriculture; recent developments in bio-technology suggest that this pattern is likely to extend into the future.

Education

An old joke in Canada is that this country is the only place in the world that speaks English without an accent—a bit of a rebuff to England's stilted tones and to the odd and baffling renderings of English in certain parts of the United States. Canada has discovered, in recent years, that there is a strong global market for Canadian English and, more generally, for Canadian education. Soaring international interest in learning English—a single Japanese company has over 250,000 students per year and close to 300 million Chinese are currently studying English—has resulted in the development of a significant international trade in English as a Second Language Training. Private companies, schools, colleges and universities have entered the sector, sponsoring everything from intense short-courses for high school students to year-long immersion offerings for university students and luxury experiences for Asian business people anxious to mix language study and recreation. Several hundred thousand visitors per year partake of this growing opportunity, their numbers swollen by new Canadians who are likewise seeking to increase their English (and, to a much lesser extent, French) language proficiency. Given that ESL students tend to spend sizable amounts of money beyond their training program, these initiatives tend to contribute substantially to regional economic development.

The market for Canadian education is much larger than ESL courses. Canadian schools, public and private, are selling their courses abroad, particularly in Asia (highlighting, in the process, the greater safety in Canada than the United States). Colleges and universities, likewise, frequent educational fairs in East and South Asia, South America, and Europe, looking for students who want both a high quality educational experience, are willing to capitalize on the very low value of the Canadian dollar, and are willing to brave Canadian weather. (Unflattering portraits of Canadian winter dominate foreign understanding of the country and harm efforts to market educational and other services internationally.) Many Canadian technical and graduate programs attract large numbers of foreign students, filling the coffers of cash starved public institutions and creating opportunities for private sector firms. The private educational field, incidentally, is not heavily regulated in Canada and there have been several embarrassing episodes involving students attracted to fly-by-night Canadian schools which were unable to deliver the promised educational services.

Selling History and Nature

Canada is one of the world's most amazing nations. The country's physical diversity is simply staggering and its vast expanses defy easy characterization. The variety of landscapes makes marketing the country's tourist potential something of a challenge, but most countries would welcome such a problem. Canadian tour operators sell the country's heritage, and entice travelers to visit Toronto, Montreal and Vancouver, where the cultural diversity and history of the country can be sampled. Travelers are offered, as well, the quaint rural realities of the Maritimes and the old-world feel of Newfoundland and rural Quebec. More often, however, they are offered Canadian landscapes and wildlife. Tourists still come to see Niagra Falls, regardless of how over-built and, at times, tacky the attractions become. They are attracted by the simple beauty of Peggy's Cove, Nova Scotia, or the red sands of Prince Edward Island (and the Japanese love Anne of Green Gables' cottage). They are sold on the fishing and hunting lodges and welcome opportunities to photograph wildlife and trek in untouched wildnerness. Germans, in particular, are taken with the wilderness experience and have become among the most common visitors to the Yukon Territory and Japanese tourists have long been enamoured with the dramatic scenery of Banff and Jasper National Parks. British Columbia markets its "Super, Natural" province with great enthusiasm, and attracts thousands of travelers to tourist sites throughout the area. Vancouver is a key port for the world-famous Alaska cruise ship industry, with most of the ships working out of the first-class facility on the city's Burrard Inlet waterfront.

The Canadian tourist industry suffers from the shortness of the season. In most areas, the high season extends from late June through to mid-September (a bit longer on the west coast, where weather stays quite reliable through to the middle of October). Canadians have done a very poor job of marketing winter experiences, partly because of the uncertainties of the season (temperatures in January in many parts of the country could range

Anne of Green Gables

Prince Edward Island is in the unique situation of building a significant tourism industry off a children's story. Lucy Maud Montgomery, an island resident, wrote a series of novels about Anne, the first published in 1908. The stories were wildly popular in their day and have remained popular thereafter. The books about the impish and strong-willed orphan are a staple for young girls across North America and have long been especially popular in Japan. Anne's "home" (she was, after all, fictitious), Green Gables, is now a major tourist attraction. A play based on the books runs all summer in the province's main theater, and the character figures prominently in PEI advertising. (And regional commerce. One firm from Atlantic Canada developed a prefabricated Anne of Green Gables house for the Japanese market.) The effort works. Cavendish, Lucy Maud Montgomery's home and the site of the Green Gables and the Anne of Green Gables store, attracts thousands of visitors each summer. Over 100,000 Japanese, most of them young women raised on a steady diet of books about Anne, visit the island each year.

from 5°C to −35°C) and because of Canadian dislike of winter. As a consequence, the country enjoys a brief and intense summer tourist season and bemoans the absence of visitors the rest of the year. There is an enormous untapped potential in the winter months, as some northern entrepreneurs have discovered by promoting Northern Lights viewing, a particular attraction to the Japanese.

Tourism is an enormous industry in Canada. The country attracts thousands of Americans to summer cabins or commercial camps across the nation, and fishing and hunting lodges are a favorite for business people. Major cities are alive with tourists in the summer months, with their hotels often filled to capacity and theme parks, national historic sites, and other attractions drawing large crowds. Tourists have fueled the expansion of restaurants in the larger centers and have helped sustain the high-end retail sector.

(A decade ago, Canadians used to line up to cross the border, heading for US shopping malls built specifically to cater to Canadian clients. The falling dollar killed that recreation and, in fact, has reversed the flow. Americans in sizable numbers now come North to capitalize on cheap Canadian prices. In eastern United States, in particular, US travel agents run buses filled with seniors up to Canada for the sole purpose of buying discount, generic drugs from Canadian pharmacies, the savings more than paying for the cost of the trip.) As the number of travelers increases—inevitably with the expansion of the Chinese, Taiwanese, and Indian middle classes—Canada's market will increase dramatically, and so will the opportunities available to Canadian tourism companies.

Clusters: Saskatoon, Montreal, Kitchener-Waterloo, Calgary

Cities and regions in Canada have worked very hard to position their communities for international competitiveness. Some of these efforts—like Saint John's attempt to sell itself as a free trade zone and a focal point for the plastics industry—have not yet taken off, despite the evident advantages that the communities possess. Other communities, however, have developed strong partnerships between industry, government and post-secondary sector and have begun to establish a national and international presence in key sectors. Kitchener-Waterloo (Ontario), for example, has built off the continued success of the University of Waterloo (and its neighbor, Wilfrid Laurier University) to establish a vibrant high-technology and information technology sector. The university's engineering, computer science and other programs are closely connected to local business operations, and the regional and provincial governments have supported the continued development of high technology activities. Dozens of small companies are created each year, capitalizing on synergies between academic research, student initiative, and business interest in high technology, positioning Kitchener-Waterloo as an important player in the information-based economy.

Saskatoon provides another illustration of university-business synergy. The largest city in Saskatchewan, Saskatoon has long been the supply center for agriculture, mining and forestry in the northern half of the province. But as each of these sectors fell on hard times, local officials sought to develop a new commercial image for the city. Sizable provincial investments in the University of Saskatchewan's College of Agriculture, including a state of the art research and teaching complex and substantial funding for research, emerged as the cornerstone of an expansive and aggressive bio-technology industry. When the government and university opened Innovation Place, on the University campus, the center attracted numerous bio-technology and information technology companies, each anxious to capitalize on the connections between industry and primary research. The federal government recently joined in the initiative, funding a major sychlotron accelerator program, which adds to the research intensiveness of the University and the city. Saskatoon has done an excellent job of redirecting its economy, maintaining traditional ties (to agricultural), building on a local resource (the University), and developing a region-wide initiative in bio-technology that holds considerable promise for future economic development in the area.

Ten years ago, the thought that Montreal would emerge as a leader in the new economy would have been laughable. The threat of Quebec separation pulled the business community into the doldrums and limited the attractiveness of local investments. Business and government initiatives, involving both the provincial and federal governments (which are often at political odds with each other), overcame the politically-inspired lassitude. In recent years, Montreal has become a hive of high-technology activity, in such areas as chemicals, pharmaceuticals, aerospace technology, and information technology. The city's universities—Montreal has among the highest percentage of university students in its population of any center in North America— feed into this largely French-Canadian commercial innovation. The vitality of Montreal's business community has begun to attract back some of the companies and industries lost in the early years of the separatist movement. (Ironically, the growth of globalization and the subsequent downgrading of the role of national governments in economic affairs appears to have convinced investors that Montreal and Quebec investments would be secure whether or not the province stays within Canada.) Montreal is something of a commercial sleeper, less well-known than other Canadian centers for its business ability and yet possessed with considerable verve and determination. Moreover, French-Canadian university graduates, technicians, scientists and business people are not as likely to flee the country for other opportunities or to head to the United States. (France, incidentally, is something of an option for the cultural and intellectual elite in the province, but does not hold great attraction for the average Quebecois.)

Calgary, Alberta is, as of 2000, the country's most economically dynamic city. After suffering through a sharp depression in the early 1980s—something that the region and province continues to blame on the federal government and, by extension, central Canada—the city has rebounded with a vengeance. While current prosperity rests in part on the vitality of the oil and gas industry — Calgary is the hub of investment, exploration and development activity in this key sector—the local economy continues to expand in other areas. It is, for example, a leading center in mobile telephone technology, an area that holds enormous promise for the future. Calgary's advantages are several-fold: a low tax environment, a stunning physical setting (only a short drive from the Rocky Mountains), a free-wheeling, entrepreneurial business community, and an intense amount of civic pride. Calgarians work together — most famously on the Calgary Olympic Games of 1988—and are quick to mobilize community resources to capitalize on opportunities. Calgary has a strong oil and gas sector and has worked hard to broaden the base of its activities in this area. More importantly, the city retains a self-confidence, brashness and determination that is likely to ensure its continued prosperity.

Global Cities: Toronto and Vancouver

Canada is home to two of the world's most impressive cities. Both Toronto and Vancouver are, by global standards, safe, clean, attractive, dynamic, and culturally-aware. They boast strong commercial attributes, but vary dramatically. They differ, in particular, in the reaction of other Canadians to their success. Vancouver is chided for its laid-back, relaxed approach to life—lacking the dynamism of Calgary and the solidity of Toronto. But the city is at the top of the list of places Canadians want to live. Toronto, in contrast, is the butt of endless jokes and put-downs; hatred of Hog-Town (it used to be a major meat processing center) is a unifying factor in Canada. Canadians move here for jobs, opportunity and income, but they claim to do so reluctantly, pledging to return to the regions when opportunity strikes. They rarely do, for Torontonians are extremely proud of their city and its accomplishments.

The port city of Vancouver, nestled under the mountains and blessed with hundreds of parks, hiking trails and beaches, provides superb air connections to cities around the world, particularly to Asia, and offers a rich and diverse multicultural population. The city's stunning physical location makes it one of the most beautiful cities in the world, rivaling, if not surpassing, such places as Sydney, Australia and Buenos Aires, Argentina. Vancouver has a complex local economy: high technology, entertainment, tourism, resource development, finance, and industry. It is an important trading center and this role is likely to expand in future years. At present, it suffers from business dissatisfaction with the provincial government (high tax rates, political scandals and government mismanagement) and labor-management relations have not always been as cooperative as they are at present. As a place to live and do business, however, Vancouver is almost without parallel. Movie stars love the city—in large part because they are permitted to roam freely through the streets and stores without being mobbed by aggressive fans. At a time when amenities and quality of life are becoming increasingly important for businesses seeking to attract top-quality employees, Vancouver is destined to emerge as one of North America's most attractive and dynamic commercial centers.

Toronto is very different and is more than simply the country's largest city. It is built on the shores of Lake Ontario and offers little physical variety. The attraction of the city rests with its bustling commercial center—the hub of business and finance in Canada—its cultural life and its ethnic diversity. Toronto is one of the most multicultural cities in the world. Its citizens speak dozens of languages and there are numerous non-English newspapers, radio stations and, more recently, television channels. Cultural diversity causes some difficulties—relations between the police and Caribbean immigrants have been problematic at times—but the city truly celebrates its ethnic character. Toronto's restaurants are probably the best in the country, and its literary, theatrical and musical life surpasses any other center in Canada. Commercial activity is vibrant, and the city is the risk-capital center for the country. It relishes its national power and dreams of becoming a truly world-class city—albeit without the social difficulties, crime rate and other troubles that plague most other major urban areas.

In Vancouver and Toronto, Canada has two cities capable of competing with the best urban environments in the world. Both centers combine personal amenities, high quality of life, commercial vitality, and a truly international outlook. Both have attracted tens of thousands of immigrants from around the world (Toronto's Italian community is one of the largest outside of Italy, and the Chinese population of Vancouver continues to rise dramatically) and have included the new arrivals in the cultural and business life of the city. Business people searching for competitive, world-class cities as a base for their operations would struggle to find any place better than either of these centers.

Successful business entails prescience as much as it does an understanding of contemporary realities. Canada's current strengths are relatively evident, as are those sectors threatened by globalization and international competition. The country's full potential remains substantially untapped. Canada's access to the US market, global connections, rich resources and natural beauty, well-trained workforce and the like make for a potent combination. That the country is so open to international business creates additional opportunities, both for the country and its potential partners. What Canada lacks, at present, is either the speculative nature that fuels the United States' growth or the deeply ingrained entrepreneurship which underlies the Asian economic miracle in recent decades. The country is gradually making the shift from a government-driven economy, buttressed by a strong state-owned sector, to a more private enterprise, international business culture. The transition is underway, creating critical openings for business people who believe in the nation's potential.

Basic Facts and Travel Tips

Canada is a large and complex country. It is not a particularly difficult or formal business culture, and foreign business people will discover that Canadian business practices are informal, practical, and easily understood. The complexities of Asian business, formalities of British practices, US-style bonhomie, or European rigidity will not be encountered in Canada. Conversely, Canadian business people tend to be used to working with colleagues from around the world—a natural consequence of a high level of foreign ownership—and adapt well to different social and cultural environments. International business travelers will find the country easy, clean, safe, logical, and well-served; there are no health precautions that need to be taken. (Canadian hospitals still tend to provide medical care first and worry about payment later, thus providing a measure of assurance for travelers.)

The Canadian "Style" of Business

Canadian business people are not overly aggressive or intimidating. The general approach to business is relaxed, professional and very earnest. Canadians want to do business, are determined to sew up deals, but will not push too hard or too fast to get a final agreement. They are very open to working with people from other cultures and will probably impress you with their generosity of spirit. They most certainly do not appreciate being mistaken for Americans, and are sensitive to the suggestion that Canada is "just like" the United States. As a country, Canadians have a wicked sense of self-deprecation, however, and they will often lead the way in criticizing Canada. Note that satire is a particularly well-developed trait in the country.

There are a few other general Canadian characteristics worth keeping in mind. Canadians do not like pushy people and are willing to wait their turn. Ostentatious displays of wealth are not appreciated. Courtesy is normal—expect people to hold the doors for you and will deal with you in a very polite and friendly manner. For some, particularly Americans, Canadians can seem a little stuffy and constrained at times; they generally relax over time and become quite outgoing. French Canadians are more exuberant and outgoing. Canadians—except for French Canadians—are not prone to outward displays of affection. French Canadians will hug and kiss in public; most other Canadians protect their private space and appreciate others respecting their comfort zone. Do not expect strong arguments or loud behavior. Canadians dislike public conflict and prefer to deal with confrontations in private.

One of the most successful Canadian retailers in recent years has been Future Shop, a nationwide chain of electronics and home entertainment stores. The firm has grown to over 80 stores in the past twenty years and has established itself as a market leader in the highly competitive electronics field. The company has recently opened an internet shopping site. (www.futureshop.ca) in an attempt to compete with American dot. com retailers

Punctuality

Canadians are not time-obsessed, but they do expect business meetings to start on time. (They can, at the same time, be extremely forgiving for weather-induced delays or problems relating to traffic in the major cities. Try to phone ahead if you are going to be late.) Most Canadian businesses are open between 9:00 a.m. and 5:00 p.m. (although retail stores often have extended shopping hours). For social engagements, there is more flexibility. People generally expect visitors to arrive approximately 15 minutes after the appointed hour. Canada is not a 'late-night nation'. Most restaurants and bars will close before or shortly after midnight.

Salutations

Most Canadian business partners will quickly move to a first-name basis, but it is best not to assume this. Begin your pleasantries with full attention to their last names—ie. Mr. Smith (do not address them by their working title, ie. President Smith) for men or, for women, Ms. Smith. When dealing with French Canadians, use Monsieur (for men) and Madame (for women). People greatly appreciate the proper pronunciation of their names—and given Canada's multicultural nature, this can be a challenge at times. Do not be afraid to ask for assistance in pronouncing a difficult name. People will appreciate you making the effort. Follow your Canadian partner's lead in shifting to a first name basis—and realize that Canadians will generally be comfortable with either continued formality or informality. So, if you are used to a more formal style of business salutations, they will typically be fine with that approach.

Gift-Giving

Canadian business people often exchange gifts with international partners. They are not into ostentatious presents, and typically provide something with a local connection (aboriginal crafts, for example). It is common to exchange gifts at Christmas time;

Canadian businesses will often send presents (food, liquor, or something with the company logo) to major business partners. If you have been invited to a Canadian business person's home—a common occurrence—it is appropriate to bring wine, flowers, or candy.

Business Attire

Canadian business attire is in a state of flux, but it is best to lean toward the traditional. Suit and tie (for men) and formal business suits and dresses (for women) are still the norm, but some Canadian businesses are shifting to more informal office settings. (This is especially true in the youth-oriented high technology sector.) Many offices have "Casual Fridays," when employees are encouraged to dress down for the day (often providing a small charitable donation for the privilege.) Be careful about over-dressing if you are working in a rural or northern area; locals tend to be quite scathing in their dismissal of the "suits." Also, make sure you plan for cold weather. Having a proper jacket, boots, hat and gloves is both appropriate and wise. You will not impress your business partners if you are walking around outdoors in winter in a suit jacket and oxfords.

Small Talk

Any country has its list of topics to avoid and topics to embrace. The list for Canada varies from region to region, but here is a quick "do and do not" selection. Feel free to talk about the weather, sports (particularly hockey), Canadian or American football, Canada's place in the world, world famous Canadian performers, US movies, guns control in the United States, the role of Toronto (if you are not there), the state of the Canadian health care system, and the shortcomings of politicians. Avoid talking about the value of the Canadian dollar, Quebec separation, political developments in Europe or Asia (most people pay little attention), Canadian's distaste for winter, aboriginal land and treaty rights, Canadian movies, gun control in Canada, Canadians attitudes toward Toronto (if you are there), immigration policy, and the brain drain to the United States.

The Business of Socializing

Canadians operate on an extended work day, and breakfast, lunch and dinner meetings are considered fair game for discussions. Let the Canadian business person set the tone for the meal, but do not be surprised if Canadian counterparts launch into business work over bacon and eggs, continue through a working lunch, and finalize the deal over dinner. (And note, as well, that most Canadian cities offer excellent restaurants, so you will likely be well-fed as you talk.) Feel free, by the way, to indicate your food preferences when dining; people will not be insulted if you indicate a desire for a specific kind of food (or wish to avoid what everyone else is eating). An increasing number of Canadians do not smoke (and many restaurants have large no-smoking sections). Also, drinking heavily is no longer very common in Canadian business settings. Remember that Canadian businesses add a 7% GST to restaurant bills—and that tipping is expected (10%–15% is normal, and a higher rate is expected in top-flight restaurants).

Business Cards

Business cards are typically exchanged (in a less ceremonial fashion than in Asia) at the time of first meeting. Note that many North Americans now use electronic devices to store business information; do not be surprised to see someone pull out a small computer to check personal information and contact details.

French-English

Canada is a bilingual country and this reality should be respected. In much of Canada—particularly west of Ontario—this is rarely a big issue (and some people are not pleased with official bilingualism). In Quebec and Ontario, demonstrating an awareness of the French-English situation is appreciated; showing an understanding of Quebec's political aspirations and goals would be helpful. For dealings with Quebec business people and federal officials in Ottawa, the nation's capital, expect that your counterparts will speak French (and English) and recognize that they would appreciate an indication on your behalf of the importance of the French language. A translated business card, for example, would be useful.

Practicalities of Doing Business in Canada

The major challenge of working in Canada have to do with the size and diversity of the country. The following information is provided as a guide to Canadian business practicalities.

Languages

English is by far the most common language spoken in Canada. In Quebec, most business and government people speak both English and French. French is also spoken extensively in New Brunswick, eastern Ontario and the Winnipeg area. French translators can be quickly located in any Canadian town or city. Other than new immigrants, few Canadians speak languages other than English. Many Asian-Canadians and European-Canadians can trace their ancestry back three or more generations; few of the younger people speak the language(s) of their parents and grandparents. In the major Canadian cities, it is fairly easy to locate speakers/translators who are able to assist with business activities.

The Canadian accent, incidentally, is generally quite easy to follow and does not have the inflections, odd words and other affectations that can make British, Australian, or New Zealand English difficult to understand. There are some regional dialects (Newfoundland and Cape Breton Island are the most distinctive), but the diversity is not as pronounced as in the United States.

The general flatness of the Canadian dialect has created a substantial global demand for Canadian teachers of English as a Second Language.

Time Zones

Canada has six time zones and, except for the province of Saskatchewan and Nunavut, goes on daylight saving time. The time zones are as follows, with the deviation from Eastern time noted.:

Newfoundland and Labrador:	Plus 1 1/2 hours
Atlantic (Nova Scotia, Prince Edward Island and New Brunswick):	Plus 1 hour
Eastern (Quebec, all by the extreme western portion of Ontario, Nunavut):	——
Central (western Ontario, Manitoba and Saskatchewan):	Minus 1 hour, except for Saskatchewan in the summer months, when it is minus 2 hours.
Mountain (Alberta, western Northwest Territories, northeastern British Columbia):	Minus 2 hours
Pacific (British Columbia, except for the northeastern corner):	Minus 3 hours

Currency and Banking

Canadian business is done in Canadian dollars. Some commercial outlets will take US dollars, but be careful about the exchange rates. In the past, visitors have complained about the low exchange rates provided at restaurants, shops and other outlets. Recognizing the bad press that comes with such poor service, most retail outlets now post the exchange rate prominently, to avoid misunderstanding, and many offer very competitive rates. If in doubt, have the currency exchanged at a bank. Currency exchange services are also available at the international airports and in select locations (those with high tourist traffic) in the major cities. Do not expect to be able to use foreign currency (other than US dollars) in Canadian stores, restaurants or outlets. (There are a few exceptions. Tourist hotels in Banff and Jasper, Alberta, make a special effort to accommodate Japanese visitors and some will accept payment in yen.)

Canada has an excellent banking system, consisting of a series of national bank networks (Toronto Dominion, Royal, Scotiabank, Montreal Canadian Bank of Commerce), several international banks (HSBC has the most extensive network) and numerous trust companies and credit unions. The banking system is very advanced technologically. Point of sale electronic services are available at almost all stores, restaurants and hotels. Major credit cards can be used across the country. Canadians, in fact, are among the world's greatest users of automated banking (including internet banking). Automatic Teller Machines (ATMs) can be found throughout the country, including at banking offices, department stores and malls, gasoline stations and convenience stores. There are a growing number of "cash machines," which are not operated by a specific bank and which charge substantial transaction fees. This being Canada, however, consumers are warned about the fees and given a chance to abort their transaction should they wish to.

Air Travel

Until early in 2000, Canada had two major airlines—Air Canada (a former state-owned enterprise) and Canadian Airlines International. After a bitter fight for market share that left CAI in desperate financial shape, Air Canada took over its former competitor. The national airline system is now being "rationalized," and Canadian travelers are not pleased. Many scheduled flights have been canceled, seat sales have declined, and according to most, service has suffered. Air Canada, always a tad more imperious than its western rival, has become more so since the merger. The airlines management has claimed to have made a concerted effort to improve service, but Canadians are skeptical that a veritable monopoly will provide competitive prices and a high level of customer satisfaction. Air Canada, incidentally, is linked to the global Star Alliance and provides lovely business class lounges in all of the major airports.

There is some competition for Canadian travelers' dollars. WestJet, based in Calgary, Alberta, offers cheap flights, prompt service and a customer-first mentality (and a pop and peanuts approach to in-flight meals). The company had expanded operations into Ontario to fill the void left by the departure of Canadian Airlines. Westerners will back the upstart, as they sided with Canadian Airlines in the past, and it appears to be on a strong financial footing. Eastern Canada, particularly Atlantic Canada, is served much less well. There are several charter and new scheduled airlines operating out of Halifax, Moncton (the most active airport in New Brunswick) and St. John's, but the other communities are not well served. Also, it is not clear how many of the airlines will be able to compete over the long-term with Air Canada. (Canada 3000 appears to be the best bet, for those looking for cheap flights and willing to put up with a restricted schedule and less than stellar in-flight amenities.)

Other Travel Options

In a sentence, there are not very many. Canadians, like Americans, are addicted to their vehicles and a great deal of government money goes into building freeways and expressways. For travelers, rent-a-car service is available at airports, from major hotels and through downtown outlets. Cars can be rented very inexpensively, but travelers are cautioned to check their insurance coverage to ensure that they are protected against future charges in case of an accident. Most travelers will rely on taxis to get from the airport and to move around the cities. In some Canadian centers, the taxis are an embarrassment—ill-kept, poorly maintained, and driven by people who have made little effort to provide a professional appearance. Some cities have tightened up taxi regulations (particularly for airport pick-up). The quality of taxi service in Toronto and Vancouver is much better than in the past; other centers have a long way to go.

There are some transit services available. Montreal and Toronto have good subway systems—but most commuters still use their cars. Edmonton and Calgary offer light rapid transit services in select areas, but they are not overused. Vancouver is expanding its Skytrain network, but it does not serve many of the most heavily populated areas. There is a reasonable Go-Train, or commuter train, service in southern Ontario, which has aided the spread of Toronto's suburbs, and Vancouver runs a heavily subsidized rail service to the eastern suburbs and a fascinating water ferry service to the North Shore—the latter offering the cheapest and one of the best sightseeing trips in Canada. Urban buses provide reasonable service in the larger cities, but usage is quite small and the buses are substantially subsidized. There is a bus service connection to almost all of the towns in the country—and this is a great way to discover just how very large Canada is. Bus travel is very time-consuming, and, given the availability of discount airlines, not always much cheaper than flying.

Rocky Mountaineer

In the heyday of train travel, Canadian railways were the backbone of the nation's transportation system. The advent of automobile and aeroplane travel undercut the viability of train travel. There are few passenger routes still operating in Canada and, outside the Toronto region, poor schedules have deterred all but the most intrepid rail travelers. The boom in Canadian tourism has, however, resulted in an upsurge in luxury train service in Canada, particularly in the mountainous regions of British Columbia and Alberta. Beginning some ten years ago, Rocky Mountaineer Ltd. introduced sightseeing trains onto the Vancouver-Banff and Vancouver-Jasper routes, attracting a large and enthusiastic clientele to their summer schedule (recently expanded to include several winter trips). The high-end service has drawn tourists from around the world, offering both luxurious facilities, the breathtaking scenery of the western mountains, and a reconstruction of old-time rail travel. In a country where passenger trains have all but ceased operations, the success of tourist travel keeps alive an industry that was once at the heart of the Canadian transportation sector.

Hotels

International travelers will be well-pleased with the quality and variety of hotel accommodation available in Canada. There are a series of major international and national chains offering top-flight rooms and services in most of the larger cities. The chains include Hilton, Delta, Hyatt Regency, Radisson, Marriott, Ramada, Westin, Intercontinental, Sheraton, Canadian Pacific (some stellar properties with old-time charm). For those working on a smaller budget—and the larger hotels are not expensive by global standards—there is a second-tier of business hotels and motels, including Travelodge, Holiday Inn, Country Inn and Suites, Days Inn, Quality Inn, Comfort Inn, Howard Johnson, Best Western, etc. The best deal for long-term travelers can be found in the many suite hotels opening up in the major cities. These properties offer large, comfortable rooms (usually with a separate bedroom and kitchen facilities) close to downtown businesses. Canadian cities also offer bed and breakfast accommodations and, for those remaining for a time in the area, long-term rental properties.

Business Services
Canadian cities are generally well set up for business travelers. While amenities may be a little short in the smaller centers, travelers can usually find short-term office rentals, temporary office help, and business equipment centers (fax, computer, printer and other services). In fact, most major hotels provide all of these services within the property. Internet centers are not very common at present and are aimed more at the cappuccino crowd than at business people.

Food/Dining Out
Any traveler holding on to stereotypes about Canada as a cultural backwater and frontier society is in for a very pleasant surprise. The large immigrant population in the country has ensured that a wide variety of restaurants are available in all Canadian cities. And Canadians have responded by patronizing the dining rooms, and ensuring the continued operation of first-class restaurants. Montreal's dining is simply superb, and the service personnel are among the most knowledgeable and professional in the country. Toronto and Vancouver offer remarkable ethnic diversity, and wide price ranges. Each of these cities is home to dozens of top quality restaurants—with excellent meals available at respectable prices. A stroll through the downtown areas in any major city will reveal many high quality (and numerous inexpensive) restaurants. Ask for recommendations—and check out one of the national or regional restaurants. Some of the results are to be expected. The steaks in Alberta are as good as advertised, British Columbia offers excellent seafood and has the best Asian cooking in the country, Prince Edward Island does a mean lobster, the Caribbean, Italian

and Greek food in Toronto is sensational, and it seems as though everyone in Montreal and Quebec City knows how to produce gourmet cooking. Others will be a surprise. Who would expect to find one of the very best East Indian restaurants in the country to be in Saskatoon, excellent Thai dining in Saint John, New Brunswick, a wonderful Italian meal in Prince George, British Columbia, or a choice of first-rate Vietnamese restaurants in Ottawa, once the killing ground of Canadian fine dining! Outside of Halifax and, to a lesser extent, St. John's, Newfoundland, choices are thinner on the ground in the Maritimes, but central and western Canada are notable for the diversity, quality, and price competitiveness of its restaurants.

Recreational Facilities

Visitors looking for a break from business will find many opportunities across the country. The larger cities have excellent live entertainment (music, theater, dance) and each hosts several performing arts theaters. There are first-rate festivals located across the country, ranging from the Jazz festivals in Montreal and Vancouver to Toronto's Harborfront literary events and Edmonton's remarkable folk and fringe festivals. Canadians are very enthusiastic moviegoers. The main cities have art and foreign film offerings; the other cities have a less diverse fare (but check around the universities if you are looking for something other than the latest Hollywood blockbuster). Television service is among the best in the world, with cable systems delivering a bewildering array of program choices at surprisingly low prices. Most hotels offer premium television packages, which will provide fifty or more channels.

Considerable efforts have been made to tidy up the downtown areas in the cities and to provide additional amenities for residents and visitors. There are usually jogging paths/hiking trails available. Several, like the walk around the seawall in Vancouver and Montreal's Mount Royal Park, are simply spectacular; the others are attractive, and generally safe (although women walking alone at night should be very careful). Exercise facilities—swimming pools, tennis and racquet courts, fitness classes and exercise gyms—can be found in both public centers (at a low price, but usually quite crowded), semi-public operations (like the YMCA/YWCA), and private centers (more extensive, higher-end and more quiet). Again, hotels tend to have small pools and a little exercise equipment.

Major News Sources
Canadians follow current events with considerable intensity (less so than the Japanese, but much more than Americans). The major sources of news in Canada are:

Newspapers
Globe and Mail and *National Post*, both of which are available across the country. The latter is a recent upstart known for its sharp edge and conservative approach to business and government affairs. The *National Post* includes the *Financial Times;* the *Globe and Mail* includes *Report on Business*. Both provide excellent coverage of Canadian business news.

Newspaper Wars
Visitors to Canada will discover two national newspapers, engaged in a vigorous (at times bitter) struggle for attention, circulation and advertising. The *Globe and Mail* has been around for a long time, and has offered itself as the country's "national newspaper" for close to twenty years. (This means, in the main, that it is available for same day and even home delivery coast to coast, and also means that the newspaper maintains small regional bureaus.) In 1998, a new rival entered the scene, backed by the deep pockets of international media mogul Conrad Black (who owned dozens of newspapers across the country, most he has since sold, and major newspapers in England and Israel). The

National Post strove, from the beginning, to be very different. It offered a more formal format, more editorial content, arguably better writing, and a decidedly right-wing slant (with an occasional left-wing columnist thrown in for some balance). The paper attacked the Liberal government, provided extensive coverage of US issues, and supported the emergence of a "unite the right" political movement in Canada (which resulted, in 2000, in the establishment of the Canadian Alliance Party). Forecasts of the *National Post's* quick demise proved unfounded, although losses ran high in the first two years. By 2000, the two papers were extremely competitive, both in circulation and public attention. The *Globe and Mail*, once dismissive of the upstart, made substantial editorial and managerial changes, revamped the physical layout of the paper, and redeveloped major sections. The result has been better news reporting, intense competition for public attention (which, in turn, has spurred investigative journalism), and improved service to the reading public. Catch up with the battle at a Canadian newsstand or web-sit..

Magazines

MacLean's is the national equivalent of *Time* or *Newsweek*, both of which can also be found in Canadian magazine stores. *MacLean's* is published weekly and is available on newsstands throughout Canada. *Saturday Night*, included with the *National Post*, is a more reflective magazine.

Radio

The government-owned and commercial free Canadian Broadcasting Corporation provides superb regional and national programming. *This Morning*, which runs weekdays and Sundays between 9:00 a.m. and 11:00 a.m. offers an excellent introduction to Canadian affairs. The country has hundreds of rock, popular and speciality radio stations. Few make much of an effort to cover the news. Canada is, however, well-known for its talk-radio—which operates at a much more professional level than much of the material offered in the United States. Radio personalities can be extremely powerful politically and exercise considerable influence over public policy debates. The discussion is particularly lively in Montreal, Toronto and British Columbia. The best example of this approach to radio is CKNW (98 AM) in Vancouver.

Canadian Holidays

Canada has the following national holidays. On these occasions, most businesses close and there are usually many community events. If the day falls on a weekend, the official holiday is taken on the following Monday, creating a three-day weekend.

1 January, New Year's Day
April (the exact days vary), Good Friday and Easter Monday
24 May, Victoria Day
1 July, Canada Day (formerly called Dominion Day)
First Monday in August, Provincial Holiday
First Monday in September, Labour Day
First Monday in October, Canadian Thanksgiving
11 November, Remembrance Day (to recall Canada's
involvement in foreign wars)
25 December, Christmas Day
26 December, Boxing Day

Most Canadians take annual vacations in July and August, when all schools are in recess. Older Canadians have shifted their holidays to the winter months.

Canadian Facts

Population: 31,281,092 (July 2000 est.)
Birth rate: 11.41 births/1,000 population (2000 est.)
Population growth rate: 1.02% (2000 est.)
Birth rate: 11.41 births/1,000 population (2000 est.)
Death rate: 7.39 deaths/1,000 population (2000 est.)
Net migration rate: 6.2 migrant(s)/1,000 population (2000 est.)
Life expectancy at birth: total population: 79.43 years
male: 76.02 years; female: 83 years (2000 est.)
Languages: English 59.3% (official), French 23.2% (official), other 17.5%
Literacy rate: 97%
GDP—composition by sector:
    agriculture: 3%
    industry: 31%
    services: 66% (1998)

Canada's International Trade

Exports: $277 billion (f.o.b., 1999 est.)
Exports—commodities: motor vehicles and parts, newsprint, wood pulp, timber, crude petroleum, machinery, natural gas, aluminum, telecommunications equipment, electricity
Exports—partners: United States 84%, Japan 3%, United Kingdom, Germany, South Korea, Netherlands, China (1998)
Imports: $259.3 billion (f.o.b., 1999 est.)
Imports—commodities: machinery and equipment, crude oil, chemicals, motor vehicles and parts, durable consumer goods, electricity
Imports—partners: United States 77%, Japan 3%, United Kingdom, Germany, France, Mexico, Taiwan, South Korea (1998)

Population and Capital Cities

Canada (Ottawa)	30,750,000
Newfoundland (St. John's)	538,000
Nova Scotia (Halifax)	941,000
Prince Edward Island (Charlottetown)	138,000
New Brunswick (Fredericton)	757,000
Quebec (Quebec City)	372,000
Ontario (Toronto)	11,669,000
Manitoba (Winnipeg)	1,148,000
Saskatchewan (Regina)	1,024,000
Alberta (Edmonton)	2,997,000
British Columbia (Victoria)	4,064,000
Nunavut (Iqaluit)	28,000
Northwest Territories (Yellowknife)	42,000
Yukon (Whitehorse)	31,000

Source: *Statistics Canada, December 2000*

Canadian Ethnic Origins

Total population 28,528,125 (1996)

Single origins	18,303,625
British Isles origins	3,267,520
French origins	2,683,840
European origins	3,742,890
Western European origins	1,126,095
Northern European origins	167,285
Eastern European origins	867,055
Southern European origins	1,376,935
Other European origins	205,525
Arab origins	188,435
West Asian origins	106,870
South Asian origins	590,145
East and Southeast Asian origins	1,271,450
African origins	137,315
Pacific Islands origins	5,765
Latin, Central and South American origins	118,640
Caribbean origins	305,290
Aboriginal origins	477,630
Canadian origins	5,326,995
Other origins	80,840
Multiple origins	10,224,495

Canadian Price Indices

Consumer price index (1992=100)

115.0

Industrial product price index (1992=100)
129.1
Raw materials price index (1992=100)0
150.5
New housing price index (1992=100) 00   103.9
Source, *Statistics Canada,* 2000.

Labor Market Indicators

Unemployment rate (SA, percent)	6.9%
Participation rate (SA, percent)	66.2%
Employment (SA, millions)	15.0
Help-wanted index (SA, 1996=100)	181
Labor income (SA, $ billion)	45.5
Average weekly earnings (SA, $)	630.57

Note: SA = seasonally adjusted
Source: *Statistics Canada,* 2000

Educational Attainment, Canadian Labor Force, 1996

Total	
22,628,925	
Less than grade 9	2,812,015
Grades 9 to 13	9,131,775
Some postsecondary	7,684,435
University degree	
3,000,695	

Source: *Statistics Canada, 1996*

Canada at a Glance

Capital: Ottawa

Coastline: 243,791 kilometers (the world's longest)

Coldest Temperature: –63° C (–81.4° F) at Snag, Yukon, on 3 February, 1947 (For province by province cold weather records, see http://home.istar.ca/~awright/cold.html)

Distance East to West: 5,514 kilometers. North to South: 4,634 kilometers

Highest Point: Mount Logan, Yukon, elevation 5,959 meters

Hottest Temperature: 45° C (113° F) at Midale and Yellow Grass, Saskatchewan, on 5 July 1937

Largest City: Toronto, population 4,680,300 (metropolitan area, 1999 estimate)

Largest Island: Baffin Island, 507,451 square kilometers

Largest Lakes: Canadian side of Lake Huron, 36,000 square kilometers; Great Bear Lake (largest lake entirely in Canada), 31,328 square kilometers; Canadian side of Lake Superior (world's largest freshwater lake), 28,700 square kilometers

Longest River: Mackenzie River, 4,241 kilometers

Interesting Facts:

The world's highest tide is in the Bay of Fundy at Burntcoat Head, Nova Scotia (16.1 meters).

Canada contains more than half of the world's lakes.

Middle Island, Ontario, is the southernmost point in Canada. Situated in Lake Erie, it is at the same latitude as northern California.

Ottawa is one of the world's coldest national capitals (second only to Ulaanbataar, Mongolia) with an average January temperature of –11° C (12° F).

27% of Canada's land mass is north of the tree line and consists of tundra and ice caps.

Over 50% of Canadians live in only two provinces: Ontario and Quebec.

Over 90% of Canadians live 250 kilometers or less from the United States border.

Source: *Canadian Content*

Canada Compared

Human Development Index (United Nations)	1st
Freedom Country Rankings (Freedom House)	F1 (highest ranking)
World Competitiveness Ranking (International Institute for Management Development)	11th
Economic Freedom Ranking (Heritage Foundation)	Tied for 14th with Austria, Denmark, Estonia, Japan and United Arab Emirates.
Corruption Index (Internet Center for Corruption Research)	5th (behind Finland, Denmark, New Zealand and Sweden)
Risk (International Country Risk Guide)	9th
Economic Creativity Index (World Economic Forum)	15th
Environmental Regulatory Regime Index (World Economic Forum)	11th

Canadian English

allophone   someone whose mother tongue is neither English nor French

anglophone   someone whose mother tongue is English; often shortened to anglo

animator   in Quebec: an activity co-ordinator, facilitator, or radio or TV host

backbacon
(or back bacon)   Canadian bacon

bargoon   slang for bargain

beavertail   deep-fried dessert pastry resembling a beaver's tail

the Big Smoke   nickname for Toronto, Ontario

the bill   what Canadians ask for in a restaurant (Americans ask for the check)

break-up   the departure of ice in the far north

brochette   French and Quebec English for kebab

brown bread   wholewheat bread

Caisse Pop(ulaire)   type of co-op bank found mainly in Quebec

Canada Day   Canada's national holiday on 1 July (formerly called Dominion Day)

Canuck   nickname for a Canadian

the cash   the checkout counter

CEGEP (or cegep)   post-secondary junior college (pre-university) in Quebec

chesterfield   couch or sofa

clicks   slang for kilometers or kilometers per hour

Cowtown   nickname for Calgary, Alberta

deadhead   partially water-soaked or completely submerged log

deke   to get a hockey puck around an opponent by making him believe you're going the other way

dépanneur   French and Quebec English for convenience store or corner store

dossier	French and Quebec English for file or issue
Eh?	Don't you think? Huh?
elastic	rubber band
Francophone	someone whose mother tongue is French
freeze-up	the arrival of ice in the far north
Girl Guides	Girl Scouts
the Great White North	nickname for Canada
Grit	member of the Liberal Party
Habs	nickname for the Montreal Canadian hockey team
Haligonian	resident of Halifax, Nova Scotia
hang up the skates	to retire
Hogtown	nickname for Toronto, Ontario
Hollywood North	nickname for Toronto, Ontario
	Vancouver, British Columbia is a contender for this nickname
hoser	unsophisticated person
housecoat	robe or bathrobe
hydro	electricity (from the word hydroelectric)
icing sugar	powdered sugar
Indian Reserve	Indian Reservation
inukshuk	Inuit stone figure used to mark a location
Inuktitut	the language of the Inuit
Joual	This is a largely working-class French dialect spoken in Quebec. It borrows many words from English and is highly colloquial. The word *joual* is the local pronunciation of *cheval*, which means horse.
keener	boot-licker, brown-noser, suck-up, or sycophant
kerfuffle	commotion; flurry of agitation
language police	Quebec's French-language law enforcers

Leafs	nickname of the Toronto Maple Leaf's hockey team
loonie (or loony)	Canadian one-dollar coin (since 1987)
Lotus Land	nickname for Vancouver, British Columbia
mad as a wet hen	intensely annoyed
the Metro	subway in Montreal, Quebec
mickey	375 ml (13 oz) bottle of liquor
Midnight Sun	long hours of daylight in the far North during summer
mountie	member of the Royal Canadian Mounted Police
Ogopogo	legendary monster that supposedly inhabits Okanagan Lake in British Columbia
OHIP	acronym for Ontario Health Insurance Plan
péquiste (or Pequiste)	member of the Parti Québécois
permafrost	ground below the surface in the far North that never thaws
pogey	Employment Insurance (formerly Unemployment Insurance)
portage	the carrying of canoes past rapids
poutine	French fries covered with cheese curds and gravy
the Prairies	grassland; equivalent to the American Plains and the Russian steppe
railway	railroad
RCMP	Royal Canadian Mounted Police
riding	federal or provincial electoral district
the Rock	nickname for the Island of Newfoundland
running shoes (or runners)	sneakers or gym shoes
scads	many or lots
scraper	device for removing ice from car windows in winter
Screech	imported Jamaican rum popular in Newfoundland

separate schools	Roman Catholic schools in Ontario
serviette	paper napkin
Silicon Valley	nickname for Ottawa, Ontario North
The States	The United States of America
Steeltown	nickname for Hamilton, Ontario
suck (noun)	crybaby or someone who is spoiled
sugar pie	like pecan pie minus the pecans
syndicate	trade union in Quebec
table (verb)	to bring up for discussion as in a session of Parliament
tap	faucet or spigot
toonie (or twoonie)	Canadian two-dollar coin (since 1996)
toque (or tuque)	woollen, usually pointed cap worn in the winter
Tory	member of the Progressive Conservative Party
tourtière	type of meat pie
washroom	bathroom (minus the bath), lavatory or restroom
the West Island	suburbs in the western part of the Island of Montreal
Whiskey-Jack	nickname for gray jay or Canada jay (Perisoreus canadensis)
whitener	powdered non-dairy creamer put in coffee or tea
zed	the letter Z (Americans say zee)

Source: Canadian Content (http://home.istar.ca/~awright/ INDEX.HTM)

Atlantic Canada has its own regional expressions. The two most notable examples are Cape Breton Island and Newfoundland. For a fascinating guide to Newfoundland English, see http:// www.heritage.nf.ca/dictionary/default.html. A similar project on Cape Breton English is underway at the University College of Cape Breton.

Directory of Important Contacts

Canadian Business on the Web: An Internet Guide to Canadian Business

Canada is one of the world's leading Internet nations. And, if the country falls behind the United States in e-commerce retailing and digital entrepreneurship, it probably leads the United States in the availability of government and organizational information on the Internet. One can do a great deal of research on Canada from a computer terminal. The following guide is intended to provide international business people with a list of the most useful government, business and other world-wide web sites.

Business Sites
The following provide general information about Canadian business:
The Canadian Federation of Independent Business is the leading advocate for small business in Canada. Their very useful web-site can be found at (www.cfib.ca).

One of the most comprehensive business sites and an indispensable guide is Strategis (Canada's Business Information Site):
(http://strategis.ic.gc.ca)

Aboriginal Business Map (http://aboriginalmap.ic.gc.ca/) provides an excellent guide to the expanding world of indigenous business in Canada.

Canadian Business Map (http://strategis.ic.gc.ca/scdt/businessmap/engdoc/0.html). This is a superb site, with links to government offices, trade and professional associations, business directories, local and national search engines, statistical information and many other useful internet sites.

For export information, see Export Source
        http://www.exportsource.gc.ca/
and the Canadian Trade Commissioners site
        http://www.infoexport.gc.ca/

For a useful site with advice for small business and excellent contacts, see Canada Business Service Centres:
        http://www.cbsc.org/english/

For statistical information on Canadian industry sectors, see Industry Canada's site:
        http://strategis.ic.gc.ca/scdt/businessmap/engdoc/3.1.html

For trade shows in Canada, see
        http://www.expoguide.com/shows/data/loc_can.htm

For a searchable site for potential Canadian commerce partners, see Canadian Company Capabilities (http://strategis.ic.gc.ca/sc_coinf/ccc/engdoc/homepage.html) or, for a smaller listing, see http://www.marketplace.ca/

The Canadian Women's Business Network is very helpful and provides great insights in the challenges facing women in business:
        http://www.cdnbizwomen.com/

Also helpful is the Canadian Business Advertising Network
        http://www.cban.com/

Canadaone is a very useful information site for small business:
http://www.canadaone.com/

For a link site specially designed for small business in Canada, see WWW Resources for Canadian Small Business:
        http://www.corpinfoserv.com/libraries.html

For companies interested in electronic commerce for small businesses, check out the Electronic Commerce Centre's web-site:
    http://www.smallbizinfocentre.com/

For those interested in business and technology, the National Research Council maintains a very informative site:
    http://ctn.nrc.ca/

News and Business Information Sources: For those interested in monitoring Canadian affairs, the best sites are as follows:

The Globe and Mail (a major national newspaper):
    www.globeandmail.com

 The National Post (a new, major national newspaper):
    www.nationalpost.com

For a listing of other Canadian newspapers, see
    http://ajr.newslink.org/nonusnbri.html
with clickable links to many local and regional papers.

For Canadian business news, see the national newspapers.

The Globe and *Mail's Report on Business* can be found at
    http://www.robmagazine.com/
and the daily information is at
    http://www.globeandmail.com/hubs/rob.html
The National's Post's Financial Post is located at
    www.nationalpost.com
and *Canadian Business Magazine* can be found at
    http://www.canadianbusiness.com/index.shtml

For Canadian internet business news, see:
    www.canada.internet.com

For analysis of Canadian affairs from business oriented "think tanks," see The Fraser Institute (www.fraserinstitute.ca) and the Business Council on National Issues (www.bcni.com). For a different view of Canadian options, see the Canadian Centre for Policy Alternatives (www.policyalternatives.com).

Canadian Internet Portals: For general access to Canadian Internet sites, see the following sites, each of which provides very good links to Canadian sites.

> www.canada.com
> http://maplesquare.com/
> www.altavista.ca
> www.canoe.ca
> www.excite.ca

For more selective information, see the About.com network (www.about.com/aboutcanada/), which provides excellent limits to specialized moderated sites.

Government Sites: Canadian governments have made a dramatic shift to the web and provide a great deal of up-to-date information on the Internet. Many of them provide useful links to other corporate sites. The main federal government site, with links to all departments and units, can be found at http://canada.gc.ca.

The key federal government sites relating to business include the following:

Agriculture and Agri-Food Canada: http://www.agr.ca/
Atlantic Canada Oppportunities Agency: http://www.acoa.ca/
Business Development Bank of Canada: http://www.bdc.ca/
Canada Business Service Centres: http://www.cbsc.org/english/
Canada Customs and Revenue Agency: http://www.ccra-adrc.gc.ca/
Canada Economic Development: http://www.dec-ced.gc.ca/

Canadian Commercial Corporation: http://www.ccc.ca/
Canadian International Trade Tribunal: http://www.citt.gc.ca/
Canadian Radio-Television and Telecommunication Commission:
http://www.crtc.gc.ca/
Export Development Corporation: http://www.edc-see.ca/
Foreign Affairs and International Trade: http://www.dfait-maeci.gc.ca/. This is an excellent and very useful site for international business people
Industry Canada: http://www.ic.gc.ca/
National Research Council: http://www.nrc.ca/
Natural Resources Canada:
http://www.nrcan-rncan.gc.ca/homepage/index.html
Standards Council of Canada: http://www.scc.ca/
Statistics Canada: http://www.statcan.ca/
Task Force on Electronic Commerce: http://e-com.ic.gc.ca/
Western Economic Diversification Canada:
http://www.wd.gc.ca/eng/default.htm

Provincial governments are very active in business promotion. Here are the major provincial and territorial government sites. Check out the sites for business information, government contacts and commercial data. Governments in Canada are, compared to most nations, very internet-savvy.

Alberta: http://www.gov.ab.ca
British Columbia: http://www.gov.bc.ca
Manitoba: http://www.gov.mb.ca
New Brunswick: http://www.gov.nb.ca
Newfoundland: http://www.nf.ca
Northwest Territories: http://www.nt.ca
Nova Scotia: http://www.gov.ns.ca
Nunavut: http://gov.nu.ca
Ontario: http://www.on.ca
Prince Edward Island: http://www.pe.ca

Quebec: http://www.gouv.qc.ca/
Saskatchewan: http://www.gov.sk.ca
Yukon Territory: http://www.gov.yk.ca

City Sites: For travellers planning a visit to one of Canada's major cities, the following sites will provide detailed commercial, governmental, cultural and recreational information on the community. The about.com network offers more social, recreational and community information on all of the major cities in Canada.

Calgary: www.gov.calgary.ab.ca
Charlottetown: www.munisource.org/charlottetown/
welcome.html
Edmonton: www.gov.edmonton.ab.ca/
Fredericton: www.city.fredericton.nb.ca/
Halifax: http://www.region.halifax.ns.ca/
Hamilton: www.city.hamilton.on.ca/
Iqaluit: http://pooka.nunanet.com/~iqaluit/
Montreal: http://www.pagemontreal.qc.ca/eindex.html
Ottawa: http://www.city.ottawa.on.ca/
Quebec City: http://www.quebecregion.com/
Regina: http://www.cityregina.com/
Saint John: http://www.city.saint-john.nb.ca/
Saskatoon: www.city.saskatoon.sk.ca/
St. John's: www.city.st-johns.nf.ca/
Toronto: www.toronto.com
Vancouver: www.city.vancouver.bc.ca/
Victoria: www.city.victoria.bc.ca/
Whitehorse: www.city.whitehorse.yk.ca/ -
Windsor: www.city.windsor.on.ca/
Winnipeg: www.city.winnipeg.mb.ca/
Yellowknife: city.yellowknife.nt.ca/

Recommended Reading

General Reading and Background

Don Gilmour and Pierre Turgeon, *Canada: A People's History*, McClelland and Stewart, 2000.

J.R. Miller, *Skyscrapers Hide the Heavens: A History of Native-White Relations in Canada*, University of Toronto, 2000.

Desmond Morton, *A Short History of Canada*, McClelland and Stewart, 1997.

Statistics Canada, *Canada: A Portrait*, Statistics Canada, 1995.

Books on Canadian Business

Paul Beamish and A.E. Safarian, *Challenge and Response: Canadian Business in East Asia*, University of Toronto, 1999.

Rick Broadhead and Jim Carrol, *Selling Online: How to Develop a Successful E-Commerce Business in Canada*, CDG Books Canada, 1999.

Diane Francis, *Bre-X: The Inside Story*, Key Porter, 1998.

Diane Francis, *The Underground Nation: The Secret Economy & the Future of Canada*, Key Porter, 1994.

Katherine Kay, *In The Company Of Women: Canadian Businesswomen Talk About What It Takes To Create And Manage A Successful Business*, Harper Collins, 1998.

Linda McQuaig, *The Cult of Impotence: Selling the Myth of Powerlessness in the Global Economy*, Penguin, 1999.

Peter C. Newman, *The Acquisitors: The Canadian Establishment*, Penguin, 1999.

Peter C. Newman, *Titans*, Penguin, 1999.

Gordon Pitts, *In The Blood: Battles to Succeed in Canada's Family Businesses*, Doubleday, 2001.

Daniel Stoffman, *Masters of Change: Profiles of Canadian Businesses Thriving in Turbulent Times*, Brown, 1997.

Graham Taylor and Peter Baserkville, *A Concise History of Business in Canada*, Oxford, 1994.

Paul Waldie, *House Divided: The Untold Story of the McCain Story*, Penguin, 1997.

J. Whittle, *Canada Business: The Portable Encyclopaedia for Doing Business in Canada*, World Trade Press, 1996.

About the Author

KEN COATES has written widely on Canadian and Japanese issues. He is a Canadian business writer, currently working in the Kansai (Osaka) district of Japan. Together with Carin Holroyd, he has written *Pacific Partners: The Japanese Presence in Canadian Business, Culture and Society* (Lorimer, 1996) and *Success Secrets to Maximize Business in Japan* (Times Editions, 1999).

INDEX